Text by **Zonia Keywan**
Photographs by **Martin Coles**

Greater Than Kings

Harvest House
Montreal

ISBN 88772-177-X
Deposited in the Bibliothèque Nationale
of Quebec, 3rd quarter, 1977

For information, address Harvest House Ltd.
4795 St. Catherine St. W., Montreal, Quebec, H3Z 2B9

Design: Dreadnaught

Cover illustration: Studio 123, Montreal, Quebec

Printed and bound in Canada

Canadian Cataloguing in Publication Data

Keywan, Zonia, 1948 —
　　Greater than kings

Bibliography: p. vi
ISBN 0-88772-177-X

1. Ukrainians in Canada — History. 2. Land settlement — Prairie Provinces —
History. I. Coles, Martin, 1945 —　　II. Title.

FC106.U5K49　　　971'.004'91791　　　C77-00150-5

Contents

Acknowledgements

The funds that made the research for this book possible were provided by Opportunities for Youth and the Hon. Horst Schmid, Minister of Culture, Province of Alberta.

We would like to thank Dr. Manoly Lupul and Mr. Peter Savaryn for their encouragement, and Ken Predy, for his help in the first stage of our research.

We would also like to express our gratitude to the many pioneers and descendants of pioneers who so generously agreed to take the time to share their memories with us. It would be impossible to mention by name all the people who provided us with information, but we would like to single out for special thanks the residents of Smoky Lake and Willingdon, Alberta, and Sheho and Theodore, Saskatchewan, and most particularly Mr. and Mrs. John Chahley and Mr. Steve Stogrin of Smoky Lake; Miss Mary Shewchuk of Vegreville, Alberta; Mr. and Mrs. Wasyl Zazula, Mr. and Mrs. George Kowalchuk, Mr. and Mrs. Bill Shandro, Mr. and Mrs. Nick Strynadka and Mr. and Mrs. John Strynadka of Willingdon.

The following sources have provided useful information:

Czumer, W. *Spomyny* (Memoirs). Edmonton, 1942.

Diakun, Nadia Odette. "Legend of Pysanka". *Women's World*, May, 1975, 19.

Kaye, V. J. *Early Ukrainian Settlements in Canada 1895-1900*. Toronto: University of Toronto Press, 1964.

Kubijovic, V., ed. *Ukraine: A Concise Encyclopaedia, Vol. I & II*. Toronto: University of Toronto Press, 1963-71.

Lazarowich, P. J. "Ukrainian Pioneers in Western Canada". *Alberta Historical Review* 5,5 (Autumn, 1957), 17-27.

Lupul, Manoly R. "The Ukrainians and Public Education". Unpub.

MacGregor, J. G. *Vilni Zemli: The Ukrainian Settlement of Alberta*. Toronto: McClelland and Stewart, 1969.

Marunchak, Michael H. *The Ukrainian Canadians: A History*. Winnipeg, Ottawa: Ukrainian Free Academy of Sciences, 1970.

Mundare Yesterday and Today. Mundare: Basilian Fathers, 1969.

Young, Charles H. *The Ukrainian Canadians: A Study in Assimilation*. Toronto: T. Nelson, 1931.

Zonia Keywan
Martin Coles

Preface

There are in Canada today more than half a million people of Ukrainian descent. Most of them can trace their origins in this country to the land — to an isolated homestead, somewhere in the wilderness of turn-of-the-century Alberta, Saskatchewan or Manitoba, that was settled by immigrant grandparents or great-grandparents.

The earliest Ukrainian immigrants were men and women who were driven by poverty, oppression and hopelessness to turn their backs on the only world they had ever known — their native villages — and make the journey of thousands of miles to Canada, because it offered them hope for the future in the form of land enough for themselves and their children. They came to a country that was unfamiliar, a country in which they were not fully welcome, a country in which mere survival was a challenge. Yet they not only survived; they did well, and in time, turned desolate tracts of forest and marsh into the rich farmlands that now extend across the western provinces.

This is the story of the Ukrainian homesteaders: their first twenty-five years in Canada, and their struggles, individual and collective, to make the new country their home. In a large measure, it is also the story of all Canadians. With the exception of the native population, we are all descendants of immigrants who, at one time or another, ventured to the New World in search of a better way of life. The history of Canada is the sum of the stories of its many and diverse immigrants.

1 Emigration

D'Arcy McGee *Let it be the mad desire of other nations to lay waste; let it be ours to populate waste places. . . . The history of man is the history of emigration. We should look upon the emigrant, wherever born or bred, as a founder as great or greater than kings or nobles, because he is destined to conquer for himself, and not by the hands of other men, his sovereign dominion over some of the earth's surface. . . .*

"Come to Canada! Be your own master on your own land!" In the last decade of the nineteenth century the call went out throughout Europe. Scores of posters and leaflets, printed in a dozen different languages, exhorted the European peasant to give up his present life of poverty for a better future in the rich lands of the Canadian West. Canada's propaganda campaign came in the wake of the government's decision to open up the vast spaces of the western plains to immigration. This decision was the result of several contemporary events.

The construction of the Canadian Pacific Railway was finally completed. Now there was a need for a large population, and one spread out over the whole of the country, to make the new transportation system a viable economic proposition.

The expansionist tendencies of the United States had become threateningly apparent a few years earlier, when large numbers of settlers in that country had trekked westward. There had been serious talk of American annexation of a large part of the Canadian West. Canadian possession of its western land would be more secure, it was felt, if that land were more densely populated.

Furthermore, recent agricultural research expeditions conducted in the West showed conclusively that the western plains were prime agricultural land and thus a potential source of enormous wealth. The major obstacle to an early development of western agriculture was the short duration of the growing season. But the introduction of early-maturing strains of wheat — first, Red Fyfe, developed by David Fyfe of Peterborough, then Marquis — made it possible for Canada to begin exploiting that potential.

But who was going to open up Canada's millions of acres of virgin territory? The people chosen for the job would have to be willing to work extremely hard, and able to withstand a great deal of privation. For this reason, Clifford Sifton, minister responsible for immigration in the Laurier government, turned to continental Europe, and in particular middle and eastern Europe, in his search for immigrants.

True, these countries could not supply "preferred immigrants," that is, Anglo-Saxon Protestants; nonetheless, they had a rich resource that Canada needed badly at this time: a vast number of poverty-stricken peasants, whose families had worked the land for generations, and who would be tough enough to endure homesteading in the Canadian West.

To make the prospect of homesteading as attractive as possible, Canada offered these people 160 acres of land for the nominal sum of ten dollars. It was a policy designed to work to the benefit of both parties. Canada would be assured of a large supply of strong backs to turn the western soil; in return, the immigrants would have an opportunity for greater prosperity than would ever have been possible in their homelands.

The peasant farmers in the western Ukrainian provinces of Galicia and Bukovina, which were then under Austrian rule, heard the call and lost little time in taking advantage of Canada's offer. The great majority of Ukrainian peasants were born into a life of extreme poverty and oppression, for which there was no prospect of improvement. Canada offered them a hope for the future.

A driving force behind Ukrainian migration to Canada was Dr. Joseph Oleskiw, a teacher of agriculture and social activist who quickly recognized the potential of emigration to Canada as a solution to the problems of the Ukrainian peasantry. Already a small but growing number of peasants were leaving their villages, lured by recruiting agents' promises of high wages offered to workers on plantations in Argentina, Brazil and Hawaii. Many people who had no inkling of where these places were signed on blindly. But far from seeing the lavish promises fulfilled, the unfortunate emigrants found themselves used as virtual slave labour by unscrupulous landowners. Men, women and children laboured under the tropical sun for ten, twelve, fourteen hours a day for starvation wages. Unable to save enough money for the ocean passage, they could not return to their homeland. Dr. Oleskiw was convinced that Canada, by virtue of its climate and its social and political system, would be a better prospect for Ukrainians. He took it upon himself to initiate a correspondence with the Canadian Department of Immigration, in which he outlined the advantages to both sides of a large scale emigration of Ukrainian peasants to Canada. In 1895 he made an extensive tour of the Canadian prairies, and upon his return wrote a book, entitled *O emigratsii*, in which he gave detailed information about the new land to the prospective immigrant.

Dr. Oleskiw envisaged an orderly, well organized movement to Canada of small groups of suitable immigrants, each group personally supervised by himself or his associates. But it took no time at all for the emigration movement to get out of his hands. Almost overnight, as soon as word of the new ''Promised Land'' got around, emigration from Galicia and Bukovina grew to enormous proportions. Encouraged by letters from friends who had gone earlier, and by shipping agents commissioned by the Canadian government to recruit immigrants, thousands of Ukrainian peasants decided to make the break with their homeland and seek their fortunes in faraway Canada.

The decision to relocate to a foreign country halfway around the world was not an easy one to make. The age of large-scale mobility had not yet dawned. For the Ukrainian peasant to break ties with the village his family had inhabited for countless generations, to leave forever his friends and relatives, was a painful step. But the situation at home was hopeless. Desperation was powerful motivation.

Vasyl Eleniak and Ivan Pylypiw, two men from the village of Nebiliw in Galicia, are officially recognized as the first Ukrainian immigrants to Canada. They arrived in Montreal on the ship ''Oregon'' in September, 1891. Both men eventually went back for their families, and settled in Alberta, Eleniak near the present town of Chipman, and Pylypiw at Star.

Edna, or Star, as it was later called, a hamlet located forty miles east of Edmonton, was the site of the first permanent Ukrainian settlement in Canada. In the years 1892 to 1894 a number of families, who had heard Pylypiw's account of the new land when he returned to his native village, came to take up homesteads in this region. For the next twenty-five years, hundreds of settlements bearing such

In the 1890s in Galicia, the average peasant family possessed about 7.5 acres of land. The population was increasing, and with each generation the family holdings were divided among the children, so the youngsters growing up at this time could expect to own even less land than their parents.

Ukrainian names as Kiev, Lviv, Zaporozhe, Ukraina, Bukovina and many others, spread out steadily across the parkland belt of what are now the provinces of Alberta, Saskatchewan and Manitoba.

During the first few years of immigration into Canada, Ukrainians were registered under a wide variety of national categories. When registered by citizenship, they were called Austrians. When registered by province of origin, they were called Galicians and Bukovinians. Many were entered in the official records as Ruthenians, Little Russians or Poles. The term ''Ukrainian'' was rarely used before the First World War. Because of this confusion of names, the exact number of Ukrainians who came to Canada between 1891 and 1914 is not known, but it is estimated at 200,000.

Why They Came

Ivan Drohomeretsky,
"Exodus from the
Old Country,"
Manitoba, 1899; Michael
Marunchak, *The Ukrainian
Canadians: A History*
Winnipeg, 1970, p. 299.

*I once was in my native land
And I often think:
Why should I be suffering
In unhappiness?
I shall go into the wide world,
Where there's neither oppression nor lord...
But where to go? I think —
Where else but to Canada,
Where there's land and steppe
From east to west.
Oh, to Canada I'll go,
To the new land....*

A large proportion of Ukrainian peasants had no access to education. Statistics for the year 1908 showed that out of the total Galician population of 7.5 million, 4.5 million people were illiterate. Since most immigrants came from the lower strata of Galician society, it can be safely estimated that at least 60% of the immigrants were unable to read and write. (figures from Marunchak, p. 161).

The strongest motivation for Ukrainian immigrants to come to Canada was to get away. In the Ukraine of the 1890s there was much for the peasant to get away from: grinding poverty, political and national oppression by the large imperial states of Austria in the west and Russia in the east, conscription into armies of foreign powers to whom the Ukrainian people felt no allegiance.

Most Ukrainian immigrants came from the western provinces of Galicia and Bukovina, which had been swallowed up by the Austro-Hungarian empire. These provinces were severely over-populated. Enormous landholdings by wealthy landlords assured that there would be little land left over for the peasants. With each generation, every peasant family's property was divided among the children, so individual holdings grew progressively smaller. Now, the typical peasant family eked out a meagre existence on a few acres of land. Taxes were high. Wood for building and for fuel was very scarce, and thus was sold at exorbitant rates.

For the mass of the Ukrainian people, there was no hope that future generations might escape the vicious cycle of peasant life. The ruling classes, composed largely of foreigners who had no interest in the welfare of the Ukrainian peasant, saw to it that the oppressive class system was rigidly maintained. Education beyond the most elementary stages was denied to children of peasants. In some villages there were no schools at all. As a result, illiteracy was common. Many of the Ukrainians who came to Canada before the First World War were totally illiterate.

As Austrian subjects, all men of Galicia and Bukovina were inducted into the Austrian army for three years at the age of twenty-one. To avoid military service, it became common practice for young men approaching their eighteenth birthdays to emigrate to Canada, usually with their families, but sometimes alone. Once a boy turned eighteen, he would no longer be granted a passport. Austria wasn't eager to lose its future cannon fodder.

As the expectation of war in Europe grew stronger, parents of older boys often found ways to falsify their documents and send them to Canada. They didn't want their sons to die defending a foreign empire.

One, or a combination of these factors lay behind almost every Ukrainian family's decision to emigrate to Canada, the land that promised them wealth and liberty.

Father Basil   The conditions in Ukraine were terrible at that time. My father had seven children. He had five acres of land. How was he going to divide up that land among his children? It was the hunger for land and wood that drove people to Canada. Wood was so scarce, people had to divide matches into two or even four pieces before using them.

Mrs. Kowalchuk The army was the worst thing. At twenty-one every man had to go into the Austrian army for three years. Even after that, he had to go back every year for a few weeks. My father was away a lot of the time because of that. My mother was so sick of that army, she talked my father into coming to Canada.

Tom Predy In the Old Country my family had one acre of land. When they heard that in Canada they could have 160 acres, they thought they would be rich.

Mike Novakowsky My parents weren't as poor as some. They had twelve acres of land. Both my parents could read and write although they didn't have much education. My father was involved with politics. He was a radical. They came here to have the freedom they would never have at home.

George Miskey I came mainly to get away from armies and wars. My older brother was in the army. He could see that war was coming, so he told me to get away, to go to Canada. I was eighteen years old, but to get a passport I had to lie, to say I was only seventeen. So I left for Canada in the spring of 1913.

Mrs. Homeniuk My father went to Canada by himself at first. He worked in the mines. He made a lot more money there than he ever did in the Old Country, so he decided the whole family should move to Canada. When he came to get us, I didn't want to go. I was fifteen years old. My parents told me I could come and look, and if I didn't like it, I could go back. Of course, once I got there, there was no way I could go back.

The first brave souls to come to Canada ventured on their own. These few soon wrote back to friends who had stayed behind, urging them to emigrate as well. Their praises of the new land, which were, in fact, often exaggerated, made a tremendous impression on those back home. Every time a new letter from Canada arrived in a Ukrainian village, the whole population gathered together to hear it read aloud by whoever among them knew how to read. The pro-immigration message was also carried by shipping agents hired by the Canadian authorities as immigrant recruiters, who took to wandering through the countryside, spreading stories about the wonders Canada held in store.

Thus, in a matter of a few years, a raging immigration fever was generated among the Ukrainian peasantry. Once a few of their compatriots had taken the step, people who would not have dared to go earlier were preparing to leave, comforted by the expectation of finding a relative, friend, or just a fellow Ukrainian waiting for them when they arrived. Married men, attracted by the promise of a better future for their children, talked often-reluctant wives into emigrating. Young single men were lured by the prospect of well-paying jobs and the adventure of travel to a foreign land. Soon large groups of people were banding together to make the journey. For example, in 1899, thirty-two families from the village of Toporiwtsi, in Bukovina, emigrated to Canada together, and settled seventy miles north-east of Edmonton, forming the nucleus of the settlement that is now Smoky Lake. During the decade 1900 to 1910, 150 more families from Toporiwtsi abandoned their village for Canada.

Ivan Pylypiw, who, with Vasyl Eleniak, was the first Ukrainian peasant to come to Canada, was born in 1859 in the village of Nebiliw, Galicia. He died in 1936. In 1937, the almanac of the Ukrainian Canadian newspaper *Canadian Farmer* printed an interview with Pylypiw conducted five years earlier by Prof. Ivan Bobersky. Pylypiw recounts the events that surrounded his first journey to Canada:

"How the First Two Ukrainians got to Canada,"
W. Czumer, *Memoirs*, Edmonton, 1942, pp. 18-23, (author's translation).

We were the first from Nebiliw to go to Canada. . . . I went to school in the village and learned how to read and write. Our teacher used to talk about America and Canada. Later I heard more from Germans who had relatives over there. A lot of people from our village worked on log floats, and there people used to talk about Canada.

"Do you have your relatives' address?" I asked one German. He said he did.

"Write it down for me," I said. Havrey wrote down the address of his son and daughter, and I wrote them a letter. In their answer they said, "Leave all your troubles and come here." I wrote back, "I'm coming."

I was eager to go right away. . . . But my wife didn't want to leave. She was afraid of crossing the ocean and going to a foreign land. She kept saying to me every day, "I won't go, I won't go, I won't go."

"Well then, stay here," I said.

I sold a pair of horses and oxen to get the money for the trip, but that still wasn't enough, so I sold a piece of land too. . . . I went to the village office to get a passport. It wasn't easy, but finally I got one. I had them write out the passport for the whole family, including my wife and three children, but I went alone. This was in the fall of 1891.

Three of us set out together: Vasyl Eleniak, Yurko Panishchak and I. They were both from Nebiliw. Both were married, but they went without their wives, like me. Panishchak was my wife's brother. Neither he nor Eleniak ever went to school, so they couldn't read or write.

We rode to Stry, then to Peremeshel and Osvientsim. There the officials looked over our papers.

"Show us your money," one of them said. I had 600 renskys (about $240), Eleniak had 190 ($76) and Panishchak had 120 ($48). The officials said Panishchak had to go back to the village. Eleniak and I went on to Hamburg, and there an agent put us aboard a ship that was going across the ocean. We rode for twenty-two days. The ship crossed the ocean, then went up a big river to a large city — Montreal. We got off the ship in the morning, and in the afternoon we boarded a train and set out across Canada. The trip was very long. For two-and-a-half days we went through rock, forest, lakes and barren plains. We could see that this was a wild country. Finally, we arrived at some little town with wooden buildings. At the station some officials who spoke our language told us to get off. We were in Winnipeg. . . .

At the station in Winnipeg we were introduced to a man who spoke German and Ukrainian. He was supposed to show us the land. We could go anywhere we wanted by train for free. The agent first took us to Langenburg (Sask.), to visit a farmer. We stayed there for a week and I met some Germans who used to work under me in the woods back home. We liked the farms we saw in the area, so I registered a homestead in my name, and one in Eleniak's name, since he couldn't write.

We went back to Winnipeg and paid ten dollars each for the land we chose. Then I met a German who came from near our village and was now working as a shoemaker. He said to me, "In Alberta it's warmer. Go there and take a look."

So I went to the office and said that I wanted to go to Alberta. . . . We went to Calgary since there wasn't any track to Edmonton yet. We got to Grenfell (Sask.). There was land everywhere, wherever you looked, empty land just waiting for someone to pick up a plough and start working on it. It wasn't anything like the Old Country, where people sat on tiny pieces of land — some not even large enough for a garden. But we didn't see any woods here, so we went back to Winnipeg.

There we met some Russian Jews, and they said, "Go to Gretna, not far from here. There you'll find good land." We got tickets for Gretna and went to take a look. At the station we met some Germans who spoke Ukrainian. One of them took us to his place. There was a lot of food and drink. We spoke Ukrainian to the older people; the young ones already knew English. They told us that things were hard at the beginning, for the first three-four years, but then things got better. Now they were going well.

I decided to go back home and get my wife and children. Eleniak asked me to bring his wife too, while he stayed in Gretna to work. I was beginning to think it would be good to bring back more families from our village. They'd be able to get land close together, and this way they wouldn't miss the Old Country that much. . . .

I left Gretna on the first of December. On the fifteenth I set out from Winnipeg to Montreal. From there I went to Boston and waited five days for a ship. I sailed for twenty-two days to London and waited there two days for passage to Hamburg. I went through Berlin, Osvientsim, Krakow and Krekhovychi, then I hired a wagon to take me to Nebiliw. On the fourth day after Christmas I arrived at the village. This was January, 1892.

People kept asking me where I had been and what I saw. I told them all about Canada and said to them all, "Run, run from here. Here you don't have anything. There you'll have free land and you'll be your own masters."

But the people were ignorant. "It's far across the ocean," they said. Mothers burst into tears at the thought of going. They might have nine children, but they'd rather see all their children starve along with them than leave the village.

The people didn't understand that across the ocean there could be a free land without any masters. They listened to all I told them and were amazed. Rumours started going around the village that a man had come back from God knows where and wants to lead the people to some kind of America. One day the mayor, priest and village secretary came to my house. They asked me if the things I was saying were true. They spread a map out on the table and told me to stand by.

The secretary asked, "Where were you?"

"In America," I said. . . . "I went to Krakow, then Berlin and Hamburg. Then I went across the ocean to Montreal, and from there by train to Winnipeg."

I stood to one side while they looked at the map.

"Where did you go while you were there?" asked the priest.

"The country is called Canada," I answered. "I was in Winnipeg, in Calgary, in Gretna. Vasyl Eleniak stayed behind at Gretna to work on a farm."

There was nothing they could do — they had to believe me. The mayor just said, "Watch yourself."

One day after that I went to Perehinsko. A policeman saw me there, and said, "Pylypiw, watch yourself. One of these days I'm going to get you."

"What for?" I asked.

"You'll see. Just watch what you say."

In 1896 Canada launched an advertising campaign, and inundated Galicia and Bukovina with posters and pamphlets extolling the advantages of emigration. This advertisement proclaims that 200 million acres of land await new settlers in western Canada—160 acres for each homesteader! To the impoverished peasant, these figures were almost beyond comprehension.

I didn't pay any attention to him, and went into the tavern to drink some beer. People were curious; they gathered all around me. I told them everything they wanted to know, and added, "Run from here, because here you have no land. In Canada you'll have lots of land. Here you're nothing. There you'll be landowners."

Twelve families got together, ready to go. . . . They sold off their land and got their passports in order. I helped them to make arrangements, and they paid me a little for my help. I had an agreement with a shipping agent in Hamburg: if I got people for his ships, I'd get $5 per family. This sort of agreement was the normal thing in Canada — work has to be paid for. But our people were ignorant. They had never been out of the village. So when they found out that I was getting paid for my trouble, they began to talk.

Early one morning the policeman came to my door. He said, "Come to see the mayor."

I went with him. He brought my brother-in-law too, because he helped me to organize people, although he had never been in Canada himself. The mayor took our side, saying that we didn't do anything wrong. But the policeman took us to the police station in Kalush. They took our statements and put us in jail.

The next day we were taken to court. Our statements were produced, as well as letters from the agent in Hamburg saying that I would be paid for showing people the way to Canada. . . . The judge didn't have the power to let us go, and he said we'd have to go to Stanislaviv.

A policeman took us at bayonet point to the railroad station and rode with us to Stanislaviv. There we were put under arrest. Each of us was held separately.

I hired a lawyer to defend us both. At the trial we repeated our story.

The judge asked me, "What do you need land for? Don't you have enough here?"

I said, "No, we don't have enough here."

"You're convincing people to go to Canada?"

"No," I said. "They want to go of their own free will."

The judge said, "Why didn't you keep your mouth shut? Go by yourself, but don't drag other people with you. You've sold the people to a shipping agent. Our glorious emperor helped thirty families to come back from Argentina, at his own cost, and now you want him to help again if something happens to these people?"

The trial lasted about three hours. We were sentenced to one month. So I went to jail, while some people from our village went ahead to the new country. Others would go later.

When I finished my sentence I set out for Canada with my wife and our four children. The youngest, Anna, was six months old. We left in the spring of 1893. Yuriy Panishchak and his wife and two children came with us, and Stephan Chichak with his wife and four children. . . .

We went through Lavochne, Budapest, Vienna, Paris, Rotterdam; then we crossed the ocean and travelled up the river to Quebec. We went by train to Winnipeg. I left my family there in a rented house, and went to work in North Dakota.

I came back in December. . . . In Winnipeg I bought two oxen, a cow, a plough, a wagon, a sack of flour, salt and sugar and took them to the railroad station. For a fee of forty dollars I put everything onto a freight car. We rode to Edmonton, then to Bruderheim, where I took a homestead. I stayed there for six months, then I moved nearer to Star, or Edna, as it was called then. I've been on the same farm since 1903.

Preparing to Leave

Permanent relocation to a new country required extensive preparation. Once the decision to emigrate was made, each family had to find the means to scrape together a significant amount of money. There were numerous expenses to be met. First, there was the cost of the journey, by land to the port of departure, usually Hamburg, then by sea, then by land again to the chosen destination in Canada. The total travelling expenses for a family could easily come to two or three hundred dollars.

In addition, each family had to have on hand at least twenty-five dollars upon landing in Canada. This was a sort of insurance to guarantee that none of the immigrants would require immediate assistance from the Canadian government. Immigrants were also

My grandfather came to Canada prepared to build a house. He had a neighbour make him a tool chest before he left his village. So he arrived with a chest full of brand new tools.—Helen Kulka

encouraged to bring some extra cash to tide them over until such time as they could establish themselves firmly on their Canadian homesteads.

Few Ukrainian peasants had access to such large sums of money. The prospective immigrant tried to get what he could by selling his land and most of his possessions. Although land was scarce, and therefore valuable, a good price was hard to come by. His village neighbours could rarely afford to buy property. Most often, the would-be emigrant had no choice but to sell his land, at one-third to one-half its real value, to a wealthy landowner or the local innkeeper.

Peasants who were somewhat wealthier, and those who had the education and the foresight to read literature about Canada, were able to prepare themselves adequately for the move. They left their native villages with suitable provisions for homesteading, and with enough cash reserves to last for a year or more. But others set out blindly, nearly destitute, and with no clear idea of what awaited them on the other side of the ocean.

Large home-made wooden trunks were packed with all the things the immigrant family thought would be necessary for survival in the new country.

John Strynadka My parents came to Canada with two large trunks. You'd be surprised how many things they packed into them. There was a sickle, a scythe, an axe, all their bedding, pots, spindle, wool carders, oil, seeds for vegetables, hemp and poppy. They brought all their clothes. There were even enough sheepskin coats to give each of their three daughters new coats when they got married years later.

Apart from personal items, almost every family brought enough seeds to start new crops on the homestead: a few kernels of wheat, barley and oats, a handful of vegetable seeds, some potatoes. Uncertain as they were of what materials would be available in Canada, some people even went so far as to pack heavy items like millstones into their trunks. Who knew whether Canada would have the right sort of stone?

So common was it for ill-informed immigrants to weigh themselves down with unnecessary items, that one Canadian immigration official wrote in exasperation to his superior:

Commissioner of Immigration to the Deputy Minister;
V.J. Kaye, *Early Ukrainian Settlements in Canada 1895-1900*, Toronto, 1964, p. 100.

These people should be instructed what kind of baggage to take. They bring over here many useless articles, such as pieces of wood hewn out for a child's cradle, and this in itself would weigh almost fifty pounds. And there are many other articles of this sort which are absolutely useless, at least, the same things could be got here, or things to serve the same purpose, for a nominal sum. Then again, we find large bags of bread lying here at the station with very heavy charges against them.

As word of Canada flew around Galicia and Bukovina, more and more Ukrainian peasants wanted to go to the new country where land was free and every person was his own master. But if they had no property to sell, where would they get the money to pay their passage across the ocean? Mykhailo Stetsko, who homesteaded near Northern Valley, Alberta, recalls how he managed to get to Canada.

"How I Got to Canada,"
Czumer, pp. 34-40, (author's translation).

From the time I was a small boy I served at the estate of Mr. Khodorowsky in the village of Strilkiwtsi, Galicia. The master was a good man, level-headed, moderate in everything. He was Ukrainian and spoke to us in our own language. I enjoyed working for him.

In his household, like in others, the pay was miserable, hardly enough for a man and his wife to live on. Anyone who had a big family lived in poverty. But the master was a kind man, and he helped people if they deserved it.

I stayed at that estate for thirteen years, but not always under the same master. When Mr. Khodorowsky got old, he let his place to another. From that time life at the estate changed. The new master cut down the number of workers and made us work much harder than before. And he didn't pay us any more for it. It wasn't like Canada — there we worked from dawn to dusk for nothing.

It was getting more and more difficult for me. Although I was used to hard work from an early age, working for the new master was getting worse day by day. He drove people like cattle.

I was already married and had three children. We had a little house and a small garden. My father didn't leave me any money because he spent his whole life working on the estate. And my wife didn't bring me any wealth either. She came from a poor family. That's how it was in the Old Country — a rich girl wouldn't be allowed to marry a poor worker.

The years were passing, and I was growing worried about my children's future. It was all right while we were both healthy and the children were small; we could still manage. But what would happen when the children got bigger, when we had more of them? While I still worked for the old master such thoughts didn't come into my head, but ever since the new one came I wasn't satisfied with my life.

One Sunday morning in spring I finished my work and came home for breakfast before going to church. I told my wife that I was thinking of going to Canada.

She stared at me to see if I was sick. It seemed to her that I was talking in a fever.

"And do you have the money?" she asked.

"No, but I'll borrow it from someone."

"And what guarantee can you give?"

"I'll borrow it on my word of honour."

"Oh ho, and who needs your honour?" she said, and a tear ran down her face.... I didn't say anything more about Canada.

We came back from church, ate our lunch, and right away I set out for the estate. I didn't tell my wife that I was going to see the old master....

He was sitting on the veranda, smoking a pipe. He was surprised to see me coming on a Sunday. I approached him, took off my hat and bowed low, saying "Glory to Jesus," then walked up to him and kissed his hand. That was the custom: peasants kissed the hands of landowners and priests.

"What is it, Mykhailo?" he asked.

"I came to tell you that I want to go to Canada. . . ."

"You're tired of working on my estate?"

"No. If it were under you, I would have worked there all my life. But with the new master — I just can't. I want to go to Canada and be my own master."

"Do you have money for the journey?"

"No. That's why I came here to borrow a hundred."

"And what guarantee do I have that you'll pay me back?"

"I'll give you my word of honour, master, that I'll pay you back. And, God forbid, if I get sick I'll tell my children to pay you back, even after I die."

The master walked across the veranda, thought for a while, and said, "I believe you, Mykhailo. You've always been an honest worker." He went inside without saying another word. . . .

Finally, the door opened and he came out, holding a piece of paper. He handed it to me and said, "Take this paper and go to the bank in Borshchiw. They'll give you a hundred renskys (about $40). Go in good health to Canada, and if things don't go well there, come back to the village. There will always be work for you on my estate."

I was overwhelmed with happiness. I embraced the master's knees and kissed both his hands. I don't know whether I walked or ran home, but I was out of breath when I got to the house. My wife thought someone was chasing me.

Before she could say anything, I said, "See, he lent it to me."

She looked surprised. "Who?"

"The master."

"Where is it? Show me."

I put my hand under my arm and pulled out the piece of paper. She took it in her hand, inspected both sides like a buyer at a market, then looked at me and burst into such loud gales of laughter that tears ran down her face. She said "Mykhailo, I didn't think you could be so naive. The master couldn't get rid of you, so he gave you that piece of paper to get you out of his house." And she started to laugh even more.

I pulled myself together, and said, "The master never lied to anyone, and he wouldn't lie to me. He said to go to the bank in Borshchiw tomorrow, and they'll give me a hundred gold pieces." When I said this she laughed so hard she had to hold her sides. I was beginning to worry a little. What if my wife was right? But I wouldn't let myself doubt the master's word.

The next day, very early, I fed and watered the horses, then went to the village to find someone to take my place at work. I told the new master that I was going to Borshchiw, and that from the first he'd have to find someone to replace me. He didn't look very happy at this news, but I didn't care. I went quickly to Borshchiw. I found the bank, went inside and gave them the piece of paper. The cashier looked at it, verified the master's signature, and told me to sign on the other side. Embarrassed, I told him that I couldn't write. He called over another clerk and had him sign my name, then told me to make a cross beside it. This was the first time in my life that I signed with an X, and the first time in my thirty-one years that I had one hundred renskys. Later, in Canada, I would sign a lot of those crosses, and then I would understand that this was a 'cheque.'

The cashier counted out a hundred renskys in bills. I recounted them myself, tied them in a bundle, put it under my arm and headed back to Strilkiwtsi. I got home at noon and found my wife waiting impatiently with lunch. Before I even reached the doorstep, she called out, "Well, is there any money?"

I held out the bundle. "Now do you believe that the master wasn't lying to me?"

She untied the bundle, put the money on the table, then put her hands together as if to pray. "Oh Lord," she cried.

Within two weeks of the day I brought the money from Borshchiw, I was in Hamburg. This was in the month of June in 1906. . . .

There was still the money to be paid back to my master. I gave it back five years after coming to Canada. During my fifth year here I made some money on the railroad, and sold two little bulls, so I had enough to send him every penny I borrowed, with interest. In my letter to him I thanked him for his patience and generosity, and told him about my life in Canada. I don't know whether he believed me, but I told him that I had a 160-acre farm, with so much wood on it that if it was chopped into firewood it would heat a whole county in Galicia. I said I had fifteen acres ploughed, a pair of oxen, a cow, wagon, plough, harrow and sleigh, a house and five children, two of them already born in Canada. I thought this news would make him feel he did the right thing in lending me the money.

The old master is dead now, but I still tell my children about him, to let them know that there are some good people in this world.

Ukrainian immigrants arriving at Quebec.

Innocents Abroad

Immigration could be a profitable business, and there were plenty of unscrupulous people waiting in the wings for a chance to make a few dollars from this steadily growing new movement of peoples. The Ukrainian peasant wasn't wise to the ways of the world. Often illiterate, unused to questioning anyone in authority, he was a prime target for dishonest profiteers.

Profiteering in immigrants got its impetus from a recruitment agreement Clifford Sifton drew up in 1899 with Hamburg steamship companies. Under the terms of this agreement, shipping agents were to be paid the sum of five dollars for every head of a family who was recruited to Canada, and two dollars for every other family member. Not surprisingly, this commission system led shipping agents to use all the means at their disposal, honest and dishonest, to induce emigration in massive numbers.

Mr. Hushlak The immigration agents cared only about profit. They would get so much commission per head. So they gave people a wrong impression of Canada to encourage them to come. My parents were both illiterate. They thought that as soon as they came to Canada, they would be rich. Before they left, the agents showed them pictures of people who were living on prosperous farms. They didn't know that the farmers in the picture settled on clear land and had been farming for many years.

A vast number of agents proliferated in the Ukrainian countryside, including some bogus agents, men not connected in any way with shipping companies, who simply pocketed whatever money they squeezed out of gullible peasants. The agents spared no pains in selling Canada to the populace. They made false promises of lavish assistance to be provided by the Canadian government upon the immigrants' arrival in that country, and showed photographs of 'new homesteads' which were in fact farms settled for ten years or more.

The agents' only interest was to recruit immigrants. They did not care at all whether emigrating peasants were adequately prepared for the journey, whether they departed with sufficient funds on hand, or whether their impression of Canada had any connection with reality. To the chagrin of Dr. Oleskiw and others dedicated to supplying genuine advice and information about emigration, thousands of Ukrainian peasants were seduced by the sales talk of the agents and set out to Canada firmly convinced they were indeed headed for the Promised Land.

Once a peasant committed himself to emigration, there was no end to the ways which dishonest agents found to fleece him. They offered, at an enormous charge, to "arrange his affairs" and to procure a passport for him. They sold him steamship tickets at a cost double or triple their real price. At times, worthless scraps of paper were sold as tickets to the illiterate. Peasants were charged for fake medical examinations, cheated in the exchange of money, and were often forced to spend several weeks in port, "waiting for a ship," all the while paying the agent exorbitant prices for food and lodgings.

W. F. McCreary, Sifton's commissioner of immigration, uncovered such deplorable practices on the part of one Hamburg shipping agent. He wrote:

Kaye, p. 322.   *Certain Galicians in the party who arrived yesterday . . . have, upon examination, corroborated my previous suspicion that they were induced to emigrate although in destitute condition by promises of shipping agent Mr. Michael Morawec of Hamburg, who distinctly promised them not only free land, but that the Canadian government would further assist them by grants for subsistence, and by gifts of cattle and tools.*

During the sea voyage, passengers were regularly charged highly for food although meals were included in the price of the ticket. On the Canadian side of the ocean, a similar fate awaited them.

Immigrants were met at the Canadian port of entry by swindlers speaking Ukrainian, Polish or German, who would offer assistance, then proceed to charge them for routine services the Canadian authorities provided free of charge. Others took advantage of the newcomers' ignorance of English and of Canadian customs to underpay them in the exchange of currencies and overcharge them for food and other items.

John Korol   If you weren't careful, people would try to cheat you. When we arrived, my father was going to work so he paid a man to deliver some flour to the family. Well, the man took the money and he took two sacks of flour for himself. We had to go without any flour for six weeks.

Thanks to the efforts of all the profiteers, even those immigrants who had left home with a little money were often destitute by the time they set off to their homesteads.

The Journey

Steve Stogrin   I was four years old when we came, but I remember the trip even now. It took sixteen days from Hamburg to Halifax. Some people died on the ship. They just threw the coffins over the side.

George Miskey   I left my village in the spring. I had to wait in Hamburg for two weeks for a ship. I crossed the Atlantic in a freight ship. It took eleven days. It was very bad on the ship; the food was just terrible. They just gave us herrings and unpeeled potatoes. I was lucky. I heard before I left what the food would be like, so I brought my own. I also bought some extra food on the ship, but this was very expensive. Almost everybody got sick on the ship. Some died during the trip.

Immigrant memories of the ocean voyage to Canada are almost always the same. With the possible exception of very small children and adventure-loving young boys, passengers found the ship experience to be little short of a nightmare. People were crammed into ships in large numbers. The food was inedible. Sea sickness was universal. At times, death occured on board ship. After two weeks or more of often-rough passage, the immigrants stepped off at Halifax or at Quebec, weary and

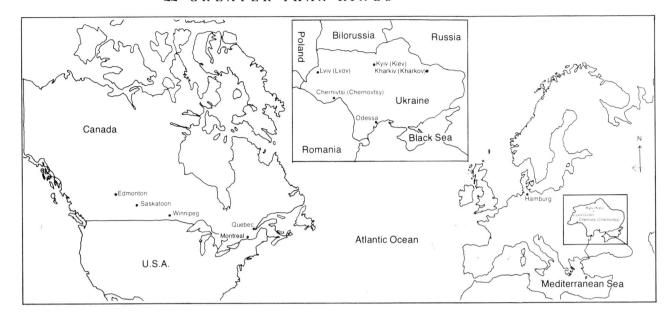

Most Ukrainian immigrants came from small villages in the region surrounding the western Ukrainian cities of Lviv and Chernivtsi. To get to Canada, they journeyed overland to a major port city—most often Hamburg, where they boarded a ship for the two or three week ocean passage to North America. They landed at the Canadian ports of Quebec or Montreal, then travelled by train to the West. From Ukrainian village to Canadian homestead, it was a journey of about 6,000 miles.

shaken, but relieved to stand once more upon solid ground.

Upon landing in a Canadian port, the immigrants were met by government officials, who checked their financial resources, and by doctors who examined them for communicable diseases. Then the second leg of the journey began, the journey by train to the prairies. The train ride of several days seemed endless to the newcomers. Canada's vastness staggered them. The long, slow ride through the rocky wasteland of the Canadian Shield disheartened many. So this was what Canadian soil was like! Would the homestead, too, be nothing but rock?

In the West, they disembarked again, at Winnipeg, perhaps, or at Edmonton. The railroad station was teeming with people speaking a multitude of languages most of which the Ukrainians did not understand. Some immigrants were met at the station by relatives or other countrymen who had come earlier. Others found their way to the large immigration halls that had been erected by the government as temporary shelters for new arrivals who had nowhere else to go. Often, men would set out immediately to search for a homestead, leaving their wives and children alone in the immigration halls for several days, or even weeks.

Bill Kereliuk   I was five years old when we came to Canada in 1902. Six families came together. We came by ship, then by train across Canada to Yorkton. In Yorkton, we stayed in the immigrant shed for six weeks while my father went to look for a homestead. We slept on the floor. We had to buy our own food. There was only one person there who knew some English, who could translate for us.

First Impressions

Immigrant poem,
Marunchak, p. 297.

Neither a path, nor a road,
Only forest and water,
Wherever we look, we see
Not our own, but foreign land.

George Miskey I grew up in a small village. I had never been away from home before I came to Canada. When I got here I was scared and confused by everything. Everything was so strange. If I could have, I would have turned around and gone straight back home.

A strong desire to turn around and go back home was the most common initial reaction to Canada. The long process of leaving their homeland, enduring the voyage by sea and by land, and finally finding themselves in a strange, foreign land, was a considerable trauma for

Newly arrived immigrants from Galicia pose for a picture at the immigration sheds in Quebec City, about 1911.

the immigrants. Now came disappointment as well. The new Promised Land did not look that good.

People who had been led to believe that streets in Canada would be almost literally paved with gold, saw immediately that this wasn't so. Meetings with countrymen often came as a rude shock when it became apparent that they were still living in poverty. These revelations resulted in disenchantment, or even anger and bitterness.

Irene Strynadka My grandfather was the first settler in his area. When another family from his village was coming, he went out to meet them. When the man from the village saw how poor my grandfather looked, how his shirt was full of holes, he said, "My God, is this how you live in Canada? Why did we come here?" He wanted to go back home.

Those who expected to find neatly laid out, comfortable farms waiting for them were quickly jolted out of that illusion.

Victoria Zaharia We came because my father's brother was here. He was always writing back to my father, saying "Come to Canada. You'll have a lot of land, wood, hay." So we came. My father took one look at all that swamp and mud and bush, and he was so angry at his brother for bringing him here. They quarreled about that for a long time.

Overwhelmed by homesickness and disappointment, many Ukrainians spent their first days in Canada in tears, wondering why they had allowed themselves and their children to be brought to this God-forsaken land. Of course, not much time could be spent in emotional self-recrimination. To go back was impossible. Most families sank every penny they had in the journey to Canada. Now they had no choice but to turn their attention to carving out a life for themselves in the new country.

Even as they set about to work, many immigrants still cherished the dream of going back home. A few did return, but the overwhelming majority stayed on. As they settled into the new routine of their lives on the homestead, as their families grew larger, the possibility of going back grew more and more remote. Nonetheless, the feeling of exile from their native land lingered with the immigrants for a long time, with some, for the rest of their lives.

Immigrant poem,
Marunchak, p. 298.

Oh, do not whisper, my grove
You green grove,
Do not give my heart more pain
Because I am in a foreign land.

It wasn't unusual for a Ukrainian family to arrive in Canada almost penniless. If newcomers were not met by friends at the train station, they might have no way of getting out to look for homesteads. For Maria Yuriychuk, later of Hamlin, Alberta, the search for homestead land was a harrowing experience.

"How We Rode by Raft to the Homestead,"
Czumer, pp. 52-55, (author's translation).

At the end of September, 1899, seven families arrived at the station in Strathcona: five from Bukovina and two of us from Galicia. The Bukovinians had some friends here, and shortly after arriving they found someone with a wagon to take them to Egg Lake, near Andrew, for a fee of fifteen dollars per family. We could have gone there too, but we didn't have enough money to pay for the ride. We only had $7.50, and we needed that for food.

Our husbands decided to look for homesteads near Edmonton. For a whole week they walked around hungry, through woods, sand and swamp, but they couldn't find any good land because there wasn't any left near the city. You had to go a hundred miles further north or east to find good land at that time.

Then the man who went with my husband met up with some friends, and took his family to stay with them. So I was left alone with

New immigrants rode to their homesteads in horse-drawn wagons or in ox-carts. Some people went on foot, carrying their possessions on their backs.

my children at the train station in Strathcona. While the other people were still with us it wasn't so bad, but when my friend left, and my husband was away for whole days at a time looking for someone who would drive us to Victoria, I was so sad I thought I'd die. I cried, and the children cried; I thought we'd go crazy with despair. Nobody would take us to Victoria. They wanted twenty dollars, and we didn't have it. Winter was coming on, and there we were with no money to live on.

Finally my husband decided to build a raft. We could float downriver to our friend Pasichny's farm. My husband was a strong and healthy Hutsul. He used to work floating logs in the Carpathian Mountains in Galicia. One time while he was in Bukovina he heard that people were going to Canada. So he decided he wanted to go too. But he didn't stop to think that it might be easy to get to Canada, but how would we live when we got there?

My husband quickly built a raft on the North Saskatchewan River, and we began to carry our bundles from the train station. It wasn't bad until it came to carrying the big trunk that held all our possessions. It weighed about 400 pounds. While we struggled with it, people gathered around to watch and laugh at us. My husband didn't know how to ask someone in English to drive it from the station. One man who noticed how we were struggling, rolling that trunk down the street, drove up to us and told us to put it on his wagon. My husband walked in front, showing him where to take it. At the river, children stood around staring at the raft. Everyone was laughing and saying, "The Galicians are going to their homestead." The driver wouldn't take any money from us. He just waved his hand and said, "Goodbye."

Around noon we started to float down the river. The next day, at dusk, we reached the ferry in Fort Saskatchewan, twenty-five miles east of Edmonton. Our raft was going very slowly. We met some Germans who spoke Ukrainian, and they told us it would take a week to get to Victoria. We had food for only two days, so my husband ran to the Fort to buy potatoes, lard and bread.

We had a tin on the raft, and we built a fire on it to bake the potatoes. My husband built a little hut on top of the raft to give us a place to hide from the rain. Our children slept there during the night. My husband and I took turns sleeping and watching the raft to make sure it didn't stray or wash up on the riverbank.

During the third night snow began to fall very thickly. We wrapped ourselves up and sat inside the little hut. Suddenly, the raft went onto the sand and stopped. We had to climb into the water barefoot, to try to push the raft back into the river, but we couldn't move it although we wore ourselves out straining at it. So we just sat on the raft until the morning. The snow was falling so hard we thought we'd be buried alive. We couldn't even light a fire because all our wood got soaked. We were so cold our teeth were chattering. I was sure that our end was near, and I cried at our misfortune and cursed my husband and his Canada.

Late in the morning some Indians looked in on us. They lived not far from the riverbank and noticed a black shape in the distance, so they came to see what was there. They took us to their little old house, warmed up some tea and gave it to us along with some dry buns. After a while we began to feel warmer. Fortunately, our children weren't as frozen as we were because they had spent the night under a big feather quilt that I brought from the Old Country. I'll never forget that night until I die. Think of it — stuck in the mud, water all around, snow coming down, and all around us wilderness. We didn't know where we were, or how far we still had to go, or where to find someone to help us push the raft back into the water. Thank God those Indians came to see who we were. If it weren't for them we would have perished there. . . .

When we warmed up a little, the Indians tried to talk to us, but we couldn't understand what they were saying. In Edmonton my husband learned to say, "I go homestead. Pasichny, Victoria." He said this to the Indians. They must have understood him, and they asked, "You Galician?" My husband didn't know what they said, but he nodded his head. They took him out into the yard and pointed at a path up a hill, saying that he should go there to see Stephan Ratsoy, Galician. They showed with the fingers on both hands that it was ten miles away. My husband did as they told him. He went to Pakan, and there the halfbreeds took him to Ratsoy, who had already been there two years and owned two horses. In the meantime, I stayed at the house with my children. The Indians had children too, and they tried to talk to mine, but they couldn't understand each other.

In the evening Ratsoy came with a wagon. My husband carried our things from the raft and we went to Pakan. Our raft stayed at Pine Creek. The next morning Ratsoy drove us twenty-five miles to Pasichny, who lived at Wasel.

Going to the Homestead

As the land in western Canada was surveyed, it was divided into townships and sections. Each township consists of thirty-six sections; a section is a square with sides one mile in length, and contains 640 acres. The homestead that was offered to new settlers for a fee of $10 was a quarter-section of land: a one-half mile square containing 160 acres. Homesteaders were free to choose their own land, but they were limited to settling on even-numbered sections. Most of the sections bearing odd numbers had been granted by the Canadian government to the CPR. In addition, the eighth and the twenty-sixth section in each township belonged to the Hudson's Bay Company, and two others were reserved as school sections. As a result, the immigrants were prevented from settling as close to each other as they might have wished.

Some Ukrainian immigrants chose to stay in the larger cities to look for work. But the majority came here to farm. For them, the first step after their arrival was to find a suitable piece of land for homesteading.

Several factors determined the choice of the homestead. A prime consideration for most people was to be near their countrymen. Some did not even inspect the available land, but simply filed on the quarter nearest to a friend or relative. Inevitably, this blind selection process resulted in some unlucky immigrants settling on worthless land. There were many cases in Manitoba, for example, of settlers struggling for years on unproductive land, then finally giving up to resettle in Saskatchewan or Alberta where the prospects for success were better.

On the other hand, the more astute immigrants went about selecting a homestead in a more methodical manner. They carefully checked all the soil in a given area until they found a piece of land to their liking.

Tom Predy   We came to Manitoba in 1899. The land there was so poor, we couldn't get anything from it. So we moved to Alberta, in 1909. When I came to take my own homestead I didn't make the same mistake. I looked around before I chose it. I dug down deep to see if the soil was good. It was good land.

In whichever of the western provinces they settled, the Ukrainians regularly chose to homestead the more northerly parkland rather than the open prairie of the south. Government officials who tried to persuade Ukrainians to go to the prairie, where far less land clearing had to be done, met with little success. Having suffered from a shortage of wood at home, the Ukrainians were determined not to do so in Canada. Settling on thickly wooded land would ensure them a constant supply of building materials and fuel for their fires.

The Ukrainians' stubborn determination to settle on the land that was most difficult to bring under cultivation evoked some scorn from other Canadians, but ultimately the choice proved to be a wise one. Parkland was less susceptible to drought than the prairie, its trees provided a natural windbreak, and the soil, when partially cleared, turned out for the most part to be productive.

Once a piece of homestead land was chosen, it was registered in the name of the head of the family. It was now his, provided that he met the government regulations of living on the land and making improvements upon it.

Before departing for the homestead, immigrants who still had some cash bought essential provisions: flour, sugar, salt, basic farming implements, and, if they could afford them, a cow and a team of oxen or horses. Those who had no money simply set off with what they had brought with them.

Steve Stogrin   We stayed at the immigrant house in Edmonton for a few days. Then we set off east, to Wostok. It took three days to get there. The men had to walk because the wagons were full of baggage and women and children. The first night we stayed with some Ukrainian people that were here before us. It was a sod hut with two rooms. Sixteen people stayed there that night.

The square grid system of surveying and allocating land that was used in western Canada was strange to the Ukrainians. In Galicia and

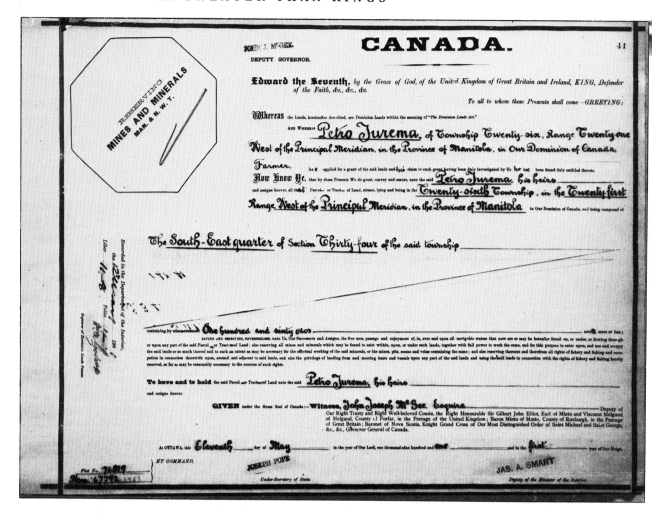

Petro Yarema, his wife Jeryna, and their four-year-old son Wasyl, emigrated from Galica to Manitoba. The family travelled to Canada on the ship SS Arcadia, which landed in Quebec on May 2, 1897.

On May 10, 1897, Petro Yarema applied for a homestead in the region of Dauphin, Manitoba. Above is his permanent title to the land, granted in 1901.

Bukovina, all the farmers in a given area lived together in villages. Each day, they went out from the villages to work on their own small pieces of land, which were located within a short walking distance from their homes.

Many immigrants had assumed that in Canada they would continue to live in the familiar village set-up. But homestead regulations required that each family live on its own separate quarter section. It was not even possible for a large number of families to take homesteads adjacent to each other, since the CPR owned every other section of land, and many sections besides were in the hands of the Hudson's Bay Company.

The Ukrainian settlers found themselves more sparsely spread out on the land than they had expected. To people used to living in close contact with their neighbours, this isolation proved to be a heavy psychological burden. Long distances between farms and lack of roads made frequent visits to friends and neighbours impossible.

A farm in Bukovina. In the background are other village houses.

Under these conditions, whatever social contacts could be maintained became all the more important. Travellers were welcomed with great hospitality, newly-arrived immigrants were readily put up in people's homes in spite of shortages of space, and occasional visits were hazarded, obstacles notwithstanding.

Fred Kopernitsky There was nothing but bush here at first. It was so dense you could easily get lost. When people went to visit each other, they would break branches to mark the way, so they could find their way back.

A lot of Ukrainian immigrants set out for Canada with no clear idea of where they were going. Pioneer settler Georgy Martyniuk tells how his group of immigrant families became victims of confusion, and almost failed to reach their intended destination in Alberta.

"Ukrainian Immigrants on the Plains of Saskatchewan on Their Way to Alberta,"
Czumer, pp. 43-46,
(author's translation).

Late in the spring of 1899 a large group of Ukrainian immigrants came by train to Winnipeg. Some people got off there, but our group of eighty families from Bukovina and half as many from Galicia were going further west, to Alberta.

We Bukovinians bought tickets in Hamburg all the way to Alberta because we knew some people there and wanted to settle close to them. Of the Galicians, some had tickets paid up for Assiniboia, others for Winnipeg. But they didn't get off the train at Winnipeg. Some stayed on because they were paid up to Assiniboia, and the rest stayed because they agreed on the ship that they'd stick with us Bukovinians all the way to Alberta, since they didn't have any friends here and didn't know where to look for homesteads.

Our train stood in Winnipeg for over an hour, then headed west. The following day, around noon, the train suddenly stopped in the middle of a wide, open prairie. Wondering what station we had come to, we hung our heads out of the window, but there was no station in sight, only a tiny hut painted red. All around there was an endless plain with a large number of gophers running across it. We had never seen such animals in the Old Country. We wondered why, although the land looked good, there wasn't a single tree growing on it, and nobody was living there.

While we were discussing this in our wagon, we suddenly heard screams and cries coming from a car ahead of us. We thought something terrible must have happened — somebody died or got sick. That was probably why the conductor stopped the train, we said to each other. But when we looked out of our windows in the direction of the noise, we saw people coming out of the train carrying their baggage and looking terribly upset, as though someone was throwing them out by force onto the prairie.

Before we could determine what was happening, the doors of our car flew open and in came some officials. They told us to get off the train. . . . Well, we were surprised because our tickets were paid for Alberta. Why were they telling us to get off?

The immigration officer said, "This is Assiniboia where you're supposed to look for homesteads."

We started to argue, saying that we didn't know anything about any "Sinaboia," but were going to Alberta, and would not get off the train. The train official became stern, like an Old Country policeman, and told us that we had to get off. We all turned to the immigration officer, who spoke Ukrainian, and accused him of betraying us, throwing us out here in this wasteland so that we'd die in a foreign land. But he just kept saying that this was "Sinaboia," and that we had to go. We were getting very angry. How could this be? We were in the middle of nowhere; there wasn't even any place to spend the night. "Who had ever heard of such a thing?" we said. . . .

The officials began to talk among themselves and walked away to the locomotive. They conferred for a long time, then detached the locomotive from our cars and rode away, leaving us on the prairie.

We figured the officials must have gone to the nearest town to telegraph to the authorities that the stubborn Bukovinians didn't want to settle on the prairie. In the meantime, we came out of the cars and sat around in a circle, like Indians, to discuss the problem. The women were crying and blaming their husbands for bringing them to Canada.

"See what has happened? Here's your Canada!" they said.

I told them not to worry. "It's not so bad," I said. "I promise you they'll come back and take us where we're supposed to go."

We sat on the prairie for more than five hours. Some of the people were crying that they came to a foreign country to die; others were laughing and joking, saying that the road to hell is easy, but the road to heaven is hard. The sun was already setting in the west, and our men in the locomotive still weren't back. We were getting ready to spend the night on the plain. Women began to feed their children and prepare the evening meal.

The children were running around happily chasing the gophers. But for us older people the hours seemed like years. In that time we had talked everything over. Some said this was some kind of fraud: the agents praised Canada in their ads, but in truth it wasn't as they said. Others thought a mistake had been made because some people had tickets for "Sinaboia." Still others thought it was part of a plan to fill the barren plains with Galicians. Well, we cursed Canada from head to toe, but I still stuck with my idea that Alberta wasn't "Sinaboia," and that it would be better in Alberta. Our friends from Banyliw wrote they had forests there, and good soil, and they never mentioned any "Sinaboia."

Late in the evening our men in the locomotive came back. They were polite to us, and said, "This was all a mistake. This train doesn't go to Alberta. Those who have tickets for Assiniboia will have to get off at the next station. The train will spend the night there, and tomorrow a freight train that's going to Alberta will take the rest of you."

So that's what happened. Early the next day the train came and our cars were attached to it. It took us all the way to Edmonton. In Alberta we felt more at home. Here we met people from our own country, and the land was better, not a desert like "Sinaboia."

We got off the train in Strathcona – South Edmonton – and spent the night at the immigration hall. On the third day we went out to look for homesteads. After two weeks I found good land near Sunland.

When we got to Edmonton, we teased the Galicians about what happened, saying "If it weren't for us stubborn Bukovinians, you'd still be in "Sinaboia" eating gophers."

Adjustments

Sawa Chernetsky-Chaly, "One Lone Cranberry;"
Marunchak, p. 301.

All is different in you, Canada!
The plants, the birds and all the animals. . . .

Life in a new country requires many adjustments on the part of the immigrant. For the Ukrainians, Canada was a whole new world in which almost everything differed from what they had known back home. Not only were Canada's language and social customs strange to them, but the natural environment as well, the climate, the terrain, the wildlife.

Mrs. Kushelic

If people knew how cold it was in Canada, I believe many would not have come. One of our neighbours wrote a letter back to the Old Country, and he said, "Canada is a fine country. We have three months of summer, and all the rest is winter."

Having come from a country with a continental climate, the Ukrainians were familiar with deep snow and cold winter temperatures. But they weren't prepared for the extreme length and severity of winter in the Canadian West. Even their thick sheepskin coats and fur hats didn't give enough protection when the mercury plummeted to minus forty degrees or lower, and bitter north winds swept across the land.

Summer, of course, was more pleasant. But even the summer weather held surprises in store.

Mike Novakowsky

One time, I remember we all went to put up a house on my father's quarter. In the evening, we were just finishing, when we saw a huge black cloud coming towards us. We were afraid. We had never seen such a black cloud before. So we all ran into the house. When that thunder and lightning started and the rain started to pour, well, I'll tell you, we never saw anything like it in the Old Country. The rain was coming right through the roof. There was mud everywhere in the house. My mother was so scared she grabbed the baby and ran to hide under the table. My father saw the cow lying in the field, and he was sure it had been killed by the lightning. We were all afraid to come out until the next morning. Then my father went out. The sky was blue, the cow was grazing out in the field. "You never know what will happen next in this Canada," my mother said.

In the hitherto unsettled bushland where most Ukrainians took up homesteads, there was an abundance of wild animals. Man's presence hadn't yet made itself felt sufficiently to drive them away. During their first few years on the land, the Ukrainian settlers frequently encountered animals of all kinds, from the bears and wolves who came to raid their food supplies, to the snakes that set up residence in their root cellars and invaded their homes. Some of the most common of western Canadian animals were entirely new creatures to the newcomers.

Mike Novakowsky   There were no skunks in the Old Country. Once I killed a skunk. I had never smelled such a terrible smell before. It made me sick for three days. So I decided to play a trick on my brother. I told him to kill a skunk because the fur was worth a lot of money. He shot one, and he got so sick! He never forgot that first lesson with a skunk.

But of all the creatures that inhabited this foreign land, the greatest scourge of all to the immigrants was the mosquito. In the bush and swamps that encircled the homesteads, mosquitoes bred by the millions. On warm summer days they swarmed at the homesteaders in such vast numbers as to make outside work almost impossible. The people did what they could to protect themselves. They burned smudges of green branches and manure, and carried them in buckets wherever they went. They even took to putting on their sheepskin coats whenever they had to step outside their doors. But all to no avail. The mosquitoes continued to torment them mercilessly. Many an immigrant who stoically endured all the other hardships imposed on him by pioneer life was driven to the end of his tether by the tiny mosquito.

Memoirs of Mikhailo Stashyn;
Kaye, p. 163.   There were such masses of them that they obstructed the view to work. If one wished to do some work outside, it was necessary to wear a face net, like the one beekeepers wear. Gloves had to be worn too. But in spite of all these precautions they still found ways to bite. They once attacked our father so badly, in spite of the heavy sheepskin coat he was wearing for protection, that his neck and throat were badly swollen and his face and ears were a shapeless mass.

The Reception

Sir Clifford Sifton *I think a stalwart peasant in a sheepskin coat, born on the soil, whose forefathers have been farmers for ten generations, with a stout wife and half a dozen children, is good quality.*

The Daily Nor-Wester, Winnipeg, December 23, 1896. *The southern Slavs are probably the least promising of all the material that could be selected for nation building.*

If Clifford Sifton recognized the value to Canada of the Ukrainian immigrant, much of the rest of the Canadian population did not. Up to this time, almost all immigrants to English-speaking Canada had been British, American or Northern European. Now the resident population didn't take kindly to the prospect of a massive influx of people from Central Europe.

No sooner did Ukrainians start coming into Canada in noticeable numbers than anti-Ukrainian sentiment began to make itself heard.

The newspapers gave the strongest voice to this new wave of public opinion. Many Canadian newspapers, including the *Edmonton Bulletin* and the Winnipeg *Daily Nor-Wester* proclaimed the racist view loudly and clearly. For example, in September, 1897, the *Daily Nor-Wester* printed an editorial which stated, in part:

The dumping down of these filthy, penniless and ignorant foreigners into progressive and intelligent communities is a serious hardship to such a community. These people . . . bring with them disease in almost every consignment . . . and their dirty habits render the stamping out of infection among them a very difficult matter. . . . They are not people who will mix socially with the English-speaking population. . . . By their unintelligent methods of farming they will lower the reputation of the products of the community . . . and their farms will be centres from which weeds and animal diseases will be disseminated in the fields and herds of their neighbours. . . . It cannot be too emphatically repeated that the people of Manitoba want no such "settlers" as these "Galicians."

Not one of the above statements about the Ukrainians was based on fact, but prejudice doesn't concern itself with facts. This editorial, and the many others like it written at the time, were simply an expression of fear, a fear of people who were different from the majority.

For the next few years, public backlash against Sifton's immigration policy grew stronger. He was accused of acting against Canada's best interest by bringing in "the scum of Europe," and was called upon in some quarters to change his policy or to resign. Even the most respected elements of Canadian society, those who should have set an example of tolerance and understanding, sometimes only added fuel to the fire of prejudice. One western Canadian religious publication referred to Ukrainians as "dirty, ignorant, garlic-smelling unpreferred continentals." Even a Member of Parliament, according to a report in the Ukrainian newspaper, *Canadian Farmer*, took time in the House of Commons to ridicule Ukrainians by reading out, in a greatly exaggerated manner, a list of "unpronounceable" Slavic names from an Alberta electoral list. The reason for his ire, it seems, was that most of the bearers of those ridiculous names had voted for the other party.

All things about the Ukrainians that were strange to Canadian eyes — their colourful homespun clothing and their sheepskin coats, their language, their customs, their Byzantine religion — were held up as proof of their inferiority. Here, for example, is one of many such cases of misunderstanding. This incident took place near present-day

Three young girls,
daughters of
homesteaders from
Bukovina, pose in their
best apparel in the
Saskatchewan bush.

Willingdon, Alberta. One Ukrainian woman was replastering the interior of her clay oven, when she heard voices, and footsteps approaching. She climbed out, dishevelled, her clothes covered with mud and clay, only to find two well-dressed gentlemen staring at her: the local school trustee and the new teacher. Ashamed of being seen in such a state, but not knowing enough English to explain what she was doing, she had no choice but to stand where she was, smiling at the strangers. The trustee looked at her with disapproval, then turned to the young teacher in his charge and said: "You see, I told you the Galicians are a dirty lot."

The most extravagant accusations were levelled against the newly-arrived Ukrainian immigrants: it was widely predicted that they would be a serious social menace; that they would lower the moral and intellectual standards of the whole of Canadian society; that they were lazy and unproductive people who would soon all become wards of the state; that they were plotting to take over the western provinces to set up their own Ukrainian state; that they were all Communists bent on destroying Canada's democratic system of government.

It was only with the passage of time, as Ukrainians showed themselves to be hard workers and dedicated farmers, that public hostility towards them gradually decreased.

But whatever progress had been made towards acceptance of Ukrainians was set back by the outbreak of the First World War. Canada was now at war with Austria, and since most Ukrainian immigrants were officially Austrian citizens, they were now regarded by the Canadian government as enemies of the state and possible traitors. All Austrian citizens were required to register as enemy aliens, and many of their rights were curtailed, including the right to Canadian citizenship, the right to travel freely, and the right to hold public gatherings in their own language. Ukrainian publications were subject to close scrutiny by government officials. Between November, 1918 and May, 1919, Ukrainian newspapers were obliged to publish bilingually, to ensure that they weren't printing any subversive material. Until the last stages of the war, Ukrainian men were not accepted into the Canadian army.

In general, farmers were left to go about their business, so long as they did so quietly, but Ukrainians living in urban centres were hounded. Anyone who failed to register with the authorities, anyone who was found to be unemployed, was sent to one of the government internment camps, located at Kapuskasing, Brandon, Lethbridge and Vernon.

The official designation of Ukrainians as enemy aliens, although unwarranted and unjust, led to their being regarded once again with

ill will and suspicion. **They were often shunned by other Canadians Some were dismissed from their jobs.**

Mike Novakowsky During the war, all aliens had to have permission to travel. An Austrian citizen didn't have the right to drive from one town to another without a permit. Once I was delivering two wagons of hay to my brother-in-law. The police stopped me and asked to see my permit. I didn't have one. So I had to go to court. I had to pay a fine of $29.00.

George Miskey If you didn't have a job during those war years you weren't safe. There were agents who would look for unemployed men all over the city. They would come and offer you coffee and say they could find you a job. Then they would send you to the work camps. You weren't given any pay there.

George Kowalchuk During the war all "aliens" had to register for a card. When they were asked, people would have to show their cards. If they had no card — off to the work camps to cut bush. But the government didn't bother us here on the farm. Later on, they took "Austrians" into the army as

(opposite)
Ukrainian homesteaders at Vegreville, Alberta, 1906. "Sifton's sheepskins" they were called. The colourful attire of the Ukrainian immigrants—and in particular their sheepskin coats—were singled out as objects of derision by Anglo-Canadians. Yet the coats were practical, ideally suited for the harsh prairie winter, and often beautifully worked with intricate decorations.

volunteers. You'd be surprised how many went. They felt they were Canadians.

Once the war with Austria was over, detainees were released from the internment camps, and things returned to their normal state. Citizenship rights were restored to Ukrainians. Ill feelings toward them began to wane.

But prejudice did not yet entirely disappear. It took a long time for Canadian people to fully accept the non Anglo-Saxon with the foreign name. For example, Ukrainians graduating from teachers' training colleges during the 1920s and 1930s had a hard time finding jobs in the cities. These good positions weren't open to "Bohunks." They had to settle for the less desirable posts in remote country schools.

It wasn't until after the Second World War, when large numbers of Ukrainians began to graduate from universities, enter all the professions, and hold offices in all levels of government, that they were at last accepted as full-fledged members of Canadian society.

2 Making a Home

Victoria Zaharia
During those first few years we were all miserable, barefoot and hungry. When we tell young people today how we used to live, they laugh at us. They say we were stupid to put up with such a life. But what else could we do — not knowing anything, not having a penny in our pockets?

If western Canada was the Promised Land, it would be some time before it fulfilled its promise to the Ukrainian immigrants. Wealth and comfort were still a long way in the future. During their initial period on the homestead, the settlers would be preoccupied with only one concern: survival.

Without a doubt, the first three or four years in the new land were the hardest. The Ukrainian peasants were hardy and resourceful people — this was, after all, why they were encouraged to come to Canada — but if ever their endurance was tried to the limit, this was the time. When, after the exhausting journey from their native provinces, they arrived at their homesteads, there was nothing to greet them but bush, mud, and the howling of coyotes at night. There was no shelter, no food, no water. Somehow, out of nothing, the settlers would have to provide themselves with the essentials of life.

In erecting the first shelter on the homestead, the only considerations were speed and ease of construction. The settlers quickly cut down a few trees and put together a log and sod-brick dugout. The dugout provided shelter from the elements — at least in times of dry weather — but it offered little comfort. Whole families spent their first few winters in Canada crowded into one tiny, dark, dingy room, cooking, sleeping and working wherever they could. During the spells of extreme cold that are so common on the prairies, the new settlers often had no choice but to stay inside for days on end. Many families arrived unprepared for the Canadian climate; they might have one pair of good boots to be shared by husband and wife, or one warm coat for three or four children.

Finding food was an ever-pressing problem. Until some land was brought into cultivation, no food could be produced on the homestead. To the extent that their resources allowed, the settlers purchased supplies of food, hauling them over great distances from Edmonton, Winnipeg or other large western centres to their isolated homesteads. But few had the money to buy all they would need to keep them alive. So they subsisted on what nature could provide: rabbits, prairie chicken, fish, wild berries and mushrooms. It wasn't enough to stave off all pangs of hunger, but at least starvation and serious illness were kept at bay.

The mammoth job for which the Ukrainians had been brought to Canada, clearing and cultivating millions of acres of western land, had yet to be tackled. During their first summer on the land, the settlers began the work that would take them many years to complete. Their progress at first was painfully slow. The immigrants couldn't afford to buy any machinery to help them in their work. Even teams of horses and oxen were beyond the means of most; they had only their own muscle power to rely upon. Armed with simple tools — axes, grubhoes, spades and hoes, the settlers began to hack out the first acre of land. They dug out trees, picked roots, hauled away heavy stones and broke the virgin soil with spades. With seeds brought over from the Old Country, they planted their first vegetable gardens. It would be a year or two before they harvested their first wheat crop, and much longer — up to fifteen or twenty years — before the whole homestead would be brought into production.

In the meantime, if the settlers were to survive, if their farms were to grow, they had to have money. Between the late 1890s and the outbreak of the First World War, thousands of Ukrainian men crisscrossed western Canada, taking jobs wherever labourers were needed: on farms, in mines, and especially on the railroads. Between Winnipeg and Edmonton, and even beyond, there was hardly a mile of new track that wasn't being laid by Ukrainian immigrants. Working outside the homesteads in such massive numbers, the Ukrainians came into wide-scale contact with other Canadians for the first time. They began to learn English and to familiarize themselves with the ways of their new country.

This one-room log shack, lost in the bush, was the first home of a settler family in Alberta.

While their husbands were away at work, the women left behind were not idle. They not only took over all family responsibilities, but continued singlehanded the grueling work on the homesteads. There was no job that was too tough for these women. Indeed, they proved they could wield an axe or a grubhoe as well as any man. Thousands of acres in the western provinces were broken for the first time by Ukrainian immigrant women.

For a few Ukrainian immigrants, the initial period of privation proved too much to bear. They abandoned their homesteads as soon as they earned the cash to pay their passage back home. But the majority hung on, clinging to the hope that the future would be easier. One thought enabled them to struggle on: however difficult their life on the land might be at the moment, it was at least their own land, and some day it would prosper. And slowly, their endurance began to pay off. Each year of working out and saving their earnings, each year of grubbing out another acre or two on the homestead, brought them closer to their goal. The first step forward came when the settlers could afford to abandon the dugout and build themselves a house. The Ukrainian thatch-roofed cottage, unique in its style, was becoming more and more visible on the face of the Canadian prairies. It was becoming clear that the Ukrainians were here to stay.

Plastered house and barn on a homestead near Smoky Lake, 1903. Most pioneer families had to endure several years in a dugout before they were able to build a house as luxurious as this one.

The First Shelter

The newly arrived Ukrainian immigrants passed their first days on the homestead making do as best they could. They slept under makeshift tents made up of wooden poles and blankets, under wagons, or just in the open air, under the stars.

As quickly as possible, each family set about erecting a shelter. Elegance and comfort were of little concern at this time. A tiny, low-ceilinged, one-room wooden shack, or a sod hut, was the best that could be expected. The most common first shelter was the sod dugout, a rough, crude structure that could be built quickly and at no cost, since all the materials were freely available right on the land.

On a clear patch of ground, the pioneer family dug a hole, two or three feet deep. Over this hole they constructed a frame, rectangular in shape and slightly higher in front than in the back, then leaned logs and branches against it to make the walls of the house. Logs piled on top of the frame made a flat, backwardly sloping roof. At the nearest slough, they cut bricks out of the soil, retaining the grass and roots, then piled these sod bricks onto the roof and the sloping walls of the house.

The dugout was tiny, rarely larger than ten feet by twelve. In front there was an opening for which a wooden door would later be made. At first, it might be left wide open, or simply curtained off with a blanket to keep out mosquitoes. A small square hole was cut in the back to serve as a window. In time, it would be filled with a small pane of glass, or just a plain white cloth.

The rough inside walls of the dugout were plastered with clay. The floor was plain dirt.

If the whole family worked briskly, the dugout would be built within a day or two.

Because it was dug deep into the ground, and its wood and earth walls were very thick, the dugout was reasonably warm in winter weather. It was also quite durable. The grass that was left growing in the sod bricks served to hold the earth together, and the sloping roof and walls of the house allowed rain water to run off, so long as the rainfall was light. When the weather turned stormy, bringing heavy rain or wind, the sod house became less secure.

Tom Predy   Our first house in Alberta had a sod roof. The third spring we lived in that house, the weather was very dry, and the roof dried out completely. When there was a strong wind, parts of the roof would blow right off.

Bill Shandro   I lived for one year in a dugout. When it rained really hard the house would just leak like crazy. It was very dark inside. There was one small glass window. The only light was from a string we dipped in coal oil and then burned. Before we had coal oil, we used animal fat.

If it offered passable protection, the dugout was far from comfortable. It was crowded, dark and dirty. Even in summer, only scant amounts of light shone through its tiny window. On winter days, after the sun had set in the afternoon, the pioneer family's only source of light was a wick burned in oil in a tin or a glass jar.

The whole family lived, ate and slept in the same room. There was far too little space for each member of the family to have a separate bed. Adults and children – whose numbers might well range up to eight or ten – slept wherever they could, most often on blankets or straw mattresses laid on the floor.

The dugout was little more than a hole in the ground, covered over with logs and earth to keep out the elements. It was erected as a temporary shelter, but for countless pioneer families many years would pass before more luxurious quarters could be provided.

Mrs. Kowalchuk   There was nothing here when my family came to the homestead. My parents built a mud dugout right away. Six people lived in it for six years. They plastered it with clay and decorated it. They slept on mattresses they made out of straw and sewed up with hemp. They covered themselves with blankets they brought with them from the Old Country.

Ann Karcha My grandparents' first "home" was about eight by ten feet. There were six people in the family, and they lived there for three years. During their third winter, my mother and her brother had to spend most of their time under a quilt in bed because they had worn out their shoes and didn't have any warm clothes left.

While the weather was warm, cooking was done outside over an open fire. But for the winter months, the pioneers had to devise a way of cooking indoors. A small, cheap tin stove often served the purpose. In some cases, the mother of the family built herself a large clay oven against one of the walls of the dugout.

Finding water suitable for drinking was a problem for many settlers.

Victoria Zaharia At first we had no well. We would take water from the slough, strain it through a cloth and drink it. I remember it was full of all sorts of little things, swimming around.

It might be some time before the homesteaders could locate a good spot on their land for digging a well. Some people were lucky enough to have a running stream on their quarter section from which they could fetch water as they needed it. Others had to walk long distances to find good water, or take their chances with what was nearby, the stagnant water in the many sloughs and small lakes that dotted the land.

Staying Alive

Building a shelter was only the first step in the struggle for survival on the new land. There was another pressing need to be met, a need that would have to be faced anew every day. How were the immigrants to feed themselves during that long period of time before their homesteads could produce any food?

Some basic supplies had to be bought in town: staples like flour, sugar, salt, coffee, tea. Those who could scrape together the price of a cow, twenty-five dollars or so, bought one immediately to assure themselves of a plentiful supply of milk, butter and cream over the first winter. Families whose financial resources were almost totally depleted by the time they got to their homesteads had to limit themselves to only minimal purchases — a sack of cheap flour, and perhaps a bag of potatoes.

For the immigrants to depend entirely on purchased food supplies was impossible, not only because they lacked the necessary cash, but because it was difficult to get to supply centres. From the outlying districts that the Ukrainians settled to the nearest large centres was often sixty or eighty miles, a distance that had to be travelled on foot, or, at best, by ox cart.

It could well take a full week for a settler to walk into the nearest town, do his shopping and return home carrying heavy sacks of supplies on his back. There were no roads for him to follow, only dirt trails made by earlier travellers. In more isolated places, he would have to make his own way through the bush. For several weeks in the spring, dirt trails turned into impassable mudholes. Rivers and large creeks could not be crossed. Under these conditions it was impossible to go for supplies more than two or three times a year.

In procuring food, as in everything else, the Ukrainians were left entirely to their own resources.

George Miskey   There was no help for people who had no money then. Nobody cared what happened to the poor. You could starve to death, and no one would help you.

Canadian government agencies of the day were not prepared to lend a helping hand to destitute immigrants. In the case of the Ukrainians they were particularly wary, being well aware of the hue and cry that would arise among Canadians were they to learn that "Galicians" were being fed at public expense. Only in the most extreme circumstances, when serious illness caused by malnutrition was discovered in some Ukrainian colonies, did the government bend its rules far enough to give the immigrants sacks of 4X flour, the lowest grade of flour that was available. No attempt was made to provide them with fresh food.

Ann Karcha   My grandparents only had a bit of flour during the first winter they were here. That was all the food they had. One of their children was sick three times during that winter from starvation. Then at Easter a neighbour gave them six potatoes to make some pyrohy. Nobody in the family ever forgot the pyrohy made from those potatoes.

Fortunately, nature was more generous than the government. The bush was teeming with wildlife, and this was where the settlers found their sustenance. During those first difficult years, partridge, prairie chicken, fish and rabbits provided the staple of their diets and kept many families from starvation.

Mary Shewchuk   If it wasn't for those rabbits and prairie chicken, many of our people would never have survived. During the first winter in Canada, most people had nothing. Nothing. My uncle lived in a dugout. He didn't even have any bullets. He had to kill prairie chicken by hitting them with his flail.

Pearl Strynadka   The rivers were so full of fish a long time ago. People could live for some time just on the fish they caught. They would weave a trap out of willows, put some bait inside, then leave it in the water. Then they'd check the trap every two or three days. Most of the time, the trap would be full of fish. Some people depended on that fish to feed their families. There was one man nearby used to catch fish on the North Saskatchewan River. He found that a neighbour was stealing fish from his trap. So he warned him, "If you steal my fish again I'll kill you." The neighbour kept stealing, so the man got so angry he killed him. He went to jail for twelve years. That's how desperate people were for food.

A gun, shells and shooting powder were the most useful items an immigrant could buy when he arrived in Canada. Many men went out hunting almost every day. Women and children set snares and wove traps for fish and small game. To a hungry pioneer family, a baked rabbit or prairie chicken tasted as good as the most sumptuous meal.

Victoria Zaharia   At first we ate rabbits a lot. My father brought a rifle with him from the Old Country. One day in winter he went out in the snow. It was very deep, up to his waist. He shot six rabbits. We skinned them, cleaned them, steamed them a little, then baked them. I remember they were so good.

Even when hunting was good, the lack of fresh vegetables was a serious problem. Small children in particular suffered from the effects of vitamin deficiency. Until they were able to plant gardens of their own, the settlers harvested what they could from the land. During the summer months the woods were full of edible wild plants and mushrooms. Everywhere bushes were laden with succulent wild berries: saskatoons, strawberries, raspberries, blueberries, rose hips. As each precious plant came into season, it was carefully picked, then dried and put away for the long winter months when no fresh food could be found.

Kost Zahariychuk, the first Ukrainian immigrant to take a homestead near Smoky Lake, Alberta, recalls how his family fared during the first year in Canada:

"The Hardships Faced by Ukrainian Colonists in Canada,"
Czumer, pp. 49-52, (author's translation).

I came to Canada with my family in the fall of 1898 from the village of Toporiwtsi, in Bukovina. We had just barely ten dollars in cash when we got to Pakan, eighty miles east of Edmonton.

I decided to go to Fort Saskatchewan to look for work on a farm. There I found a job with a German farmer, digging potatoes. In a week I earned ten bags of potatoes. To me this was a great fortune — at least I knew that we wouldn't starve to death over the winter.

When I wrote to my wife that I earned ten sacks of potatoes, she didn't believe me, but came fifty miles on foot to see for herself. The German promised me that he'd deliver the potatoes to my family after the harvest, so I buried them in the ground to keep them from freezing. To pay the farmer for delivering the potatoes, I had to plaster his barn with clay before winter came on.

But my wife couldn't wait for the delivery. She took an almost full sack of potatoes on her back and carried it fifty miles to Pakan. She came back two more times to see that the potatoes weren't frozen and that nobody stole them. Both times she tried to carry some back, but the German woman wouldn't let her, saying, "My husband said he'd deliver them, and he'll do it."

I worked for a while longer, and when the snow fell the German took me and the potatoes back to Pakan. My wife fell on her knees beside those potatoes, and prayed for an hour to thank God for not letting us die from hunger in Canada.

In the spring, when people found out that we had potatoes, they came from twenty miles away to ask for some. We gave a few to everyone. When they got them home, they cut the eyes out of those potatoes and planted them in the ground. Then they took the insides and cooked them into a broth to feed their small children. They had no milk to give them. How people suffered then! I'll never forget it until my dying day. . . .

Early in the spring of 1899 I picked out some land ten miles north of Pakan, where Smoky Lake is today. I wanted to build a dugout quickly, then go to work. For a whole week my wife and I carried our belongings through the bush from Pakan to the homestead. The worst part was carrying our old-country wooden trunk through the woods. There was no road, and it would have been impossible to get through with a wagon, so we carried it by hand.

I built a hut so that my family would have somewhere to get in out of the rain and sleep in peace away from the wild animals. There were all sorts of animals there at that time: moose, coyotes and bears.

I started walking to Edmonton and my wife stayed behind with the children. They had a sack of 4X flour, some potatoes and a piece of bacon, but no money. We had only one five-dollar bill, and I took it with me so that I'd have some money while I was travelling. There was a Hudson's Bay store at Pakan where Indians and halfbreeds traded for goods. I asked Mitchell, the manager, to give my wife food on credit — as soon as I got a job I'd pay him for it. I don't know how I convinced him, but he said he'd do it.

There were no jobs in Edmonton. On my fourth day there, I chopped some logs at a hotel and they gave me dinner, a loaf of bread, and forty cents. The next day I bought two more loaves of bread and some bacon, and went down the track south to Calgary. Calgary was a bigger and older city, I thought; there might be more work there.

Along the way I stopped at farms and asked for work. On the fourth day I got to Red Deer, one hundred miles from Edmonton. I met some Germans from Russia, and they advised me to go to Gleichen, because the farms around there were older and wealthier. So I did. I got a job with a German twenty miles north of Gleichen.

I worked there all summer and earned forty dollars in cash. The farmer also gave me an old mare and a cow. I can't tell you how I valued those animals! A rich man's millions weren't as precious to him as those two animals were to me. For four days and three nights I walked to Wetaskawin. It took a long time because along the way I had to graze the animals. By this time my provisions were gone and I was very tired, so I went to a farmer and asked for food. He saw that I could hardly stand on my feet, and that I was leading the animals, and he said to me, "You're crazy! You have a horse and you're walking. Tie the cow to the horse's tail, sit on the horse, and ride."

So from Wetaskawin I rode home on horseback. But I couldn't do this from the start because I was afraid that miserable horse wouldn't be able to take it.

When I came back to the homestead my wife got very excited. She thought that I must have stolen the animals from someone, and she began to scold me. I had to convince her that I earned them.

My wife was surprised by the cow, and I was surprised by the new house she had built over the summer with our son. It was plastered with clay inside and out, and the roof was covered with bundles of slough grass that she cut down and carried half a mile from a lake. . . .

And that's how we slowly progressed in Canada.

The First Tentative Steps

Enormous tracts of western land were waiting to be cleared, and the Ukrainian settlers quickly applied themselves to the task. Even during their first summer season on the land, most families attempted to make some inroads, however small, into transforming their home-steads into productive farmland. Their first year's progress would be miniscule. How slowly and painfully even the first acre would be hacked out of the wilderness.

To begin cultivation, the settlers chose spots where the growth was relatively sparse. From these small spots they gradually pushed out further and further.

The more fortunate immigrants were able to provide themselves from the start with a plough and a team of oxen. But a great number didn't even have that much. The first little bit of land was often carved out by the pioneers' own hands.

Every member of the family who was old enough to handle a tool joined in the work. With so much to be done, no one could be excused from work on the basis of age, sex, or physical frailty. Clearing the land by hand was a job of phenomenal proportions. What a man on a bulldozer can now easily do in one afternoon, the pioneer family would be lucky to accomplish in a whole summer of back-breaking toil.

The first step was to clear all the growth from the land. Unless they had oxen and stump pullers, the settlers did not cut down trees, for this would leave them with a stump that could not be pulled out by hand. The most common procedure was to brush the land with grubhoes, tools that were fashioned with one edge for cutting and another for digging. Armed with these useful tools, the older members of the family set about patiently digging each tree out of the ground. They dug around the base, cutting their way through the small roots, until the whole root was freed and the tree could be pulled out. It was left on the spot until the root dried out, then all the soil still adhering to the root was shaken back into the hole. The tree was now dragged off and piled with all the rest of the wood that was to be burned the following winter.

Faced with such an enormous amount of bush to clear away, the immigrants began to realize that while one can suffer from a shortage of wood, as they did back home, one can also suffer from an overabundance.

Mike Novakowsky   I was so happy when I got my quarter. I couldn't believe I could have so much land, so much bush. Anyone having so much wood in the Old Country would be a rich man. Later I realized it wouldn't be that easy to get rich. It took me three years to get used to the idea of clearing all that bush and destroying it. Wood was so precious in the Old Country.

Once the trees were cleared away, the virgin soil had to be broken, either with a walking plough, or, very often, with an ordinary spade.

The pioneer "bulldozer"
—a grubhoe.

Husbands and wives worked side by side, forcing their small spades into the hard and unyielding soil. Children helped too. Walking slowly over the land their parents had cleared, they picked off leftover roots and rocks, and broke up clods of newly-dug soil with hoes.

Needless to say, work done in this primitive fashion progressed very slowly. During their first season, a family could not expect to clear more than one-half to one acre of land. The work would continue at the rate of one to two acres per year for the next few years. It would only speed up when the immigrants acquired the money to buy more work animals and more sophisticated machinery.

Tom Predy In 1913 I took my own homestead. The quarter I took was all covered with bush. It took me from 1913 to 1928 to clear it all. The first two years I did it by hand, with a grubhoe. Then in 1915 I got horses for the first time.

During the first phase of their new life in Canada, the settlers were happy to have even a half-acre of land ready for planting. Now at least, they were able to put in a garden, and perhaps a handful of grain as well. Almost everybody had brought some seeds from the gardens they left behind in their villages. Now these seeds were put

Whole families laboured together to transform homesteads, densely overgrown with trees and bush, into arable land. This family is working on a homestead near Treherne, Manitoba.

into the ground. It was a great joy to the Ukrainian pioneers to watch their first tiny crop growing in the new land.

Pearl Strynadka The first thing they did was to plant a garden. Most people brought some seeds from the Old Country. My mother brought cabbage, carrots, beets, beans, potatoes. Some grew well here, but not all. The broad beans from the Old Country froze. And the cabbage was all green. It never had a white core. But to us it still tasted good.

Going Out to Work

At the start, most Ukrainian settlers could not afford to give all their time and energy to their homesteads. There were so many pressing needs, and so little money to pay for them. Hungry children had to be fed. Livestock and farm equipment had to be bought if work on the homestead was to progress. In almost every family, it was necessary for the father to go out to work. During their first five or ten years in Canada, most Ukrainian immigrant men regularly spent summer seasons away from home earning money, while their wives and children remained on the homesteads.

In the period before the First World War, thousands of Ukrainian

(opposite)
Ukrainian men working for
the CPR in the Crowsnest
Pass, 1909.

men were out working across the country, on railroads, on road construction, in mines, in lumber camps, on farms of wealthier settlers. Jobs were not difficult to find. The West was booming; railroads were being built everywhere. Strong-armed men were in demand. But the immigrant had to go where the jobs were.

George Miskey When I came I looked for work. First, on the railroad, on a section near Hanna, Alberta. Then I got a job with a Swede, near Wetaskawin. He hired a few young boys to cut brush with axes. Then one time I got a job building roads in the mountains. We worked until December. All this time we were sleeping in tents. It was so cold I could hardly stand it.

Shortly after his arrival in Canada, as soon as the most essential first work on the homestead was completed, the immigrant man set out to look for a job. He went alone or with a group of men from his area. He carried his clothes and some food on his back, and slept out in the bush along the way. He walked for miles, even hundreds of miles, in his search for work. From northern Saskatchewan, some men walked as far as Winnipeg, or the coal mines of southern Alberta. From Alberta, many went to British Columbia to work on mountain roads or railroads.

Eva Kretzul At first, my father used to walk to Winnipeg every year to look for work. He'd leave with 25¢ in his pocket. I remember his toes were all frozen off from the frostbite he got walking in the cold.

Fred Kopernitsky My father walked to Brandon from our farm in Saskatchewan to look for work. That was 280 miles. He got a job helping on a farm for $5.00 a month. My mother stayed behind with the children.

Eventually, the man found a job, on a work gang or on a farm. He knew no English, but chances were that wherever he worked there would be other Ukrainian men who would help him. Before long he learned enough English to understand his orders, then, to carry on a conversation. Apart from providing him with a weekly wage, working out proved very useful to the immigrant, for it gave him an opportunity to learn English. His wife, on the other hand, remained isolated on the homestead in a predominantly Ukrainian community, and often never learned any English at all.

When Ukrainian men first began to seek employment, they were met with some hostility by employers and fellow workers. But in a short space of time, they showed themselves to be good and reliable workers. Here, for example, is the opinion of Ukrainian labourers expressed by the roadmaster of one railroad company:

Robert Waters - Roadmaster, letter to C. W. Speers;
Kaye, p. 268.

Sir,

During the year just closed, 1899, I have had under me and my foreman on the M & N W Railway about 500 Galicians and Doukhobour laborers employed doing repair and construction work. About 60 percent of the above were Galicians. . . . The Galicians are first class men and have given perfect satisfaction. . . . Some of these Galicians have been with me for the last three summers. They are improving all the time. I would not want better men. . . .

One season of working out would certainly not make the immigrant wealthy. Judged by present standards, wages at the turn of the century were low indeed.

Mr. Basaraba   At sixteen I went out to work on the railroad. They paid me 15¢ an hour for a ten hour day. Then they took off 62¢ for board. When it rained we couldn't work, but still they took off the 62¢ for board.

Mike Novakowsky First I got a job in a coal mine, cutting timber for props. There were a lot of other Ukrainians working in that mine. I was paid $2.00 a day. That was a very good wage. Later I worked on the railroads. They gave me $1.25 for a nine hour day.

A man would be lucky to earn from $1.25 to $1.50 per day on a construction gang, and that sum would be reduced considerably by the time his employer deducted room and board payments. A farm labourer would get even less.

Mrs. Kowalchuk Their first summer in Canada, my father worked for a farmer. He was paid $14.00 a month. The next year, he got $15.00 a month plus two dozen eggs.

All in all, an immigrant's savings after a full season of hard work rarely exceeded sixty or eighty dollars. But of course, if wages were low, so were prices of goods. A cow might cost $25.00, a gun, $6.00, a large sack of flour, $1.25. So, although a man's earnings weren't grand by any means, his wages, if carefully spent, would enable him to put some food into the family larder, and slowly begin to outfit his farm.

Conditions of work at the turn of the century were far harsher than they are today. During the hours of work − nine or ten hours per day, six days a week − the men were expected to work, and to work hard.

Mrs. Snihor My dad worked on a railroad gang, laying ties. It was piece work. The more they got done, the more they were paid. My dad worked really fast. He was left-handed, and so he carried the ties on his left shoulder. Right until the day he died his left shoulder was lower than the right one. I'm sure it was from carrying all those ties all day long.

George Miskey At one time I had a job with the CPR. We worked for twelve hours every day, at 15¢ an hour. Our boss told us that we'd have to put in 100 new ties a day, or we'd be fired. We had to pull out the old ties, put in the new ones, spike them, trim them − 100 every day!

True, the railroads and other companies offered the immigrant labourers the convenience of room and board at the job site. But the board was not luxurious, and its price was high. In most cases, they were given as much food as they wanted, but it was plain fare indeed. A greater variety of food could be purchased from the camp canteen, but it was prohibitively expensive. The immigrants, who were obliged to save almost every penny they earned, could not afford such luxuries.

At a time when men seeking employment were in plentiful supply, and workers were not yet organized, the employer was sure to hold the upper hand. Men did as they were told, or they were dismissed from their jobs. Any employee who "caused trouble" — in some cases, merely by asking for unpaid days off on Ukrainian religious holidays — was summarily fired.

When workers attempted to organize, it was often the immigrant workers who were singled out by employers as "troublemakers." The newspaper *Svoboda* reported one such incident that took place at one of the large grain elevators in Fort William in 1906:

Marunchak, p. 211. *Fifty men were working in the elevators, including ten "Slovaks" and five "Rusyns." In order to receive a better treatment they all wanted to strike. When the dispute was over all the foreigners were fired and only the Anglo-Saxons remained at work.*

Eventually, working conditions would improve. In the meantime, most Ukrainian men worked hard and without complaint, in the knowledge that every dollar they earned represented a step forward toward establishing their families on the new homestead.

Late in the fall most men headed home, their work finished for the year. In some areas, men were able to find ways of earning cash even during the winter months.

Mrs. Snihor My family lived in Manitoba from 1899. My dad used to earn some money hauling cordwood to Neepawa, twenty-two miles from our homestead. He would sell it for 50¢ a cord. Every day in winter he piled the wood onto his sleigh and took it into town. There were many big brick houses in Manitoba at that time. People needed a lot of wood to keep them warm.

Wage earning wasn't always left solely to the father. Older children also did their share to bring in a few dollars for the needy family.

Victoria Zaharia I was a young girl, but I had to help earn some money. I would go out and help people plaster their houses for 50¢ a day.

George Kowalchuk Around 1904, 1905 some boys here would go work for the English farmers. They'd get about $3.00 a month. The parents would let them work for the English because then they wouldn't have to feed them. They'd save some money that way.

Boys were sometimes taken on as helpers on large, wealthy farms near their homes. Although not all immigrants would allow their

Coal miners—some of them Ukrainian immigrants—at Nordegg, Alberta.

daughters to work away from home, some girls found jobs as domestic workers. Many older children picked roots and rocks on neighbouring farms, plastered houses, picked berries or dug snake-root, which was dried, then taken into town markets and sold for 10¢ per pound. The young people didn't bring in much cash. Their daily earnings were rarely more than 25 or 50¢. But every penny helped in those difficult times, and there were other advantages to letting children work. Long before there were any schools in their districts, they could pick up some English from their employers, and they were often provided with full meals on the job.

Married women could not leave their children and their homesteads to work out, but even they sometimes found ways to earn a little cash. They dug snake-root on their own land, and those who were particularly skilled in handiwork sold their products to less talented neighbours.

In the spring of 1910, Nykola Virsta deserted the Austrian army to come to Canada. He was a young, single man, and before finally settling down in Bellis, Alberta, he spent nine years working all across western Canada, from the forests of western Ontario to the coal mines of British Columbia. Virsta's experience resembled that of a great number of Ukrainian immigrant men, who wandered back and forth across the West in search of jobs, and took whatever work they could find. The jobs that were open to them were unpleasant, sometimes dangerous, not always well paid, but men who had a limited command of English, and often a desperate need for money, couldn't afford to be choosy.

"My Experience in Canada,"
Czumer, pp 108-116, (author's translation).

On March 21, 1910, our ship reached St. John's, then sailed on to Quebec. There we had to pass through an inspection, to see if anyone was ill. During our passage a lot of people were sick on the ship. And the food was horrible. They gave us fish most of the time, and that made people even sicker.

To get through the inspection, you had to have $25 in cash. I was getting worried because I had only $15, and I heard people say that if you didn't have enough money, you'd get turned back. But desperation makes a man smart. I folded my single ten-dollar bill in half, and, as the inspectors walked by, I held out my money with just the ends showing, so it looked like $25. Once the inspection was over, I felt happy. Now that I was in Canada, I thought all my troubles were over.

In a few hours we got into a train and headed west. . . .

At a small station just before Winnipeg we recognized one of our countrymen getting onto the train. He had been out looking for work, but didn't find any, so he was going back to Winnipeg. We were very pleased to meet him here, since we knew that he could help us out.

Our first night in Winnipeg we slept with him on one mattress, because he had no bed in his room. The next morning we went into town to buy some food and look for work. We didn't find any, so we tried again the following day. While walking around, we came across a group of people lined up in front of an office. We could hear Ukrainian being spoken, so we went over and asked the men what they were doing.

"They're signing up workers here," they told us.

"What kind of work?"

"Ploughing with mules," they said. "The pay is $35 per month, plus board."

"That's a huge amount of money," I thought. "In the Old Country I wouldn't earn that much in half a year." So we signed up for work.

The next day we rode out by train, and by nightfall we were in a little town called Balcarres, in Saskatchewan. We walked two miles from the train station to a place filled with all kinds of wagons, ploughs and machinery, and a lot of horses and mules. This was the ranch of D. J. MacArthur, a contractor who was building new roads and railroad tracks. The next morning we went to work. All the tents and supplies were packed onto wagons, and we set out like nomads across the prairie. We rode west for eighteen miles, then set up camp beside a river. . . . We began work on a new railroad track. Some men were ploughing, others were moving earth away. A driver working with four horses or mules was paid $40 a month. The work was very hard, but the pay was good, so we stayed there for eight months, until the ground froze. I earned enough there to send $60 to my parents.

In the winter I signed up for work in the woods at Fort Frances (Ont.). The pay was $20 per month. I barely lasted one month out there — the work was very hard, and it was extremely cold. . . .

I went back to Winnipeg. On the way I saw men everywhere, wandering around looking for work, walking from one station to the next with bags slung over their backs. A lot of them had no money, and they had to walk for hundreds of miles, cold and hungry.

A few days after I got to Winnipeg, I found a job on an "extra gang." We were paid $1.25 a day, and out of that we had to pay for board. I stayed at that job for a month.

I was thinking of going to British Columbia to look for work in a mine. In the spring of 1911 I signed up for a job on a new road near Edson, Alberta. The wage was $2 a day, with $1 off for board. We took the CNR to Edmonton, then on to Edson. Between Edson and Hinton we could go at only five to ten miles an hour because of recent flooding. The train rocked like a ship all the way. We were afraid that any minute it would tip over or go off the track. But we got to Hinton safely, and went on foot for two days to where they were building the Grand Trunk Road.

They gave us grubhoes, shovels and axes, and we started cutting down trees and clearing the brush where the road was to go. It was bad; the ground was still frozen, and our foreman was a Scot who swore at us all day long. We worked for only two days, then left. On the way back we met another construction gang, and the foreman asked us to work for him. He was more humane, so we stayed there until the fall.

In the winter of 1912 I went to work in the woods west of Edson. I laboured there two months for nothing, because the contractor went bankrupt and didn't pay us. We got back to Edmonton hungry and broke.

We found a place to stay in a boardinghouse, but the rent was $20 a month, and we didn't have a penny. After searching all over the city for three days, we finally found work in a brickyard, and earned enough to pay our landlady for our board.

In the spring we went to Hinton to work on the railroad, then, in the winter, I found a job in the woods near Prince Albert, Saskatchewan. After a short time I got sick and had to go back to Edmonton. I passed the summer of 1913 doing odd jobs, then went to Brule Lake to work on railroad ties. While I was there I heard that a new coal mine had been opened up nearby, so I went there and got a job digging a tunnel into a mountain. We dynamited the rock night and day until we finally got to the coal. The tunnel was more than six hundred feet long, and there was no fresh air. The work was very dangerous. . . .

After a while I went back to Edmonton. At this time war broke out between Austria and Serbia, and all foreigners were obliged to register with the government. A friend and I found work with the Western Steel Co., but after three months they let us go, probably because we were foreigners. We went out into the country, to join some of our countrymen at Delph, Alberta. We worked on farms, helping with the threshing for 50¢ per day, and in the winter I taught Ukrainian to the farmers' children. The parents paid me 50¢ for each child every month.

In 1915 I went back to Brule Lake to work in a mine. The pit boss was a very good man, and the work went well. I stayed there for one-and-a-half years. Then I worked in other coal mines, at Yellowhead, Corbin (BC), Gibshaw, Blairmore, Rosedale and Cadomin. One time, when the coal face collapsed, I almost lost my life.

In 1919, after the war was over, I got a letter from my family back home. They said things there were even worse than they were under Austria, so I decided I'd stay in Canada for good, settle down, and get married. . . .

Women Alone

Charles H. Young, *The Ukrainian Canadians: A Study in Assimilation,* Toronto, 1931, p.88.

The average Ukrainian woman often contributes more to the work of the farm than does the average hired man. . . . The woman's labour goes far to explain the undeniable progress of the Ukrainian farmer.

While the men were away at work for months at a time, their wives stayed behind by themselves. Coping alone with life on the new homestead demanded tremendous courage and hardiness on the part of the women. Many of them were young, some just recently married. They were in a strange country, on a piece of land that was still wilderness. Communication with other settlers was slow and

difficult. There were no telephones. The nearest neighbours were a long distance away. Those women who were illiterate could not even keep in touch by letter with their absent husbands. The pioneer women were left to face not only the psychological strain of isolation, but also real physical dangers. And they had to face them alone.

Pearl Strynadka   My parents came to their homestead in summer, in June. They just put up a blanket stretched out over four posts. My mother was expecting a baby. One night, when my father was away, she could feel

A home-made wooden washboard and beating stick. On this board, the pioneer woman scrubbed her laundry; with the stick she beat the clothes as she washed them. Later, the board and stick doubled as an iron. When her clothes were almost dry, the woman wrapped them around the stick and rolled them back and forth over the smooth back of the board.

that the baby was coming. She told the other children to stay under the blanket, then she began walking the cattle trail to the neighbours' house for help. But it was dark and it was raining hard. Soon she saw that she was lost. She was so scared! She thought both she and the baby would die. All the time she was walking she was praying that she would get back home. Then she saw the blanket. She was so happy! So there she had her first baby born in Canada — in the rain, under four posts and a blanket.

Anastasia Zazula   There were lots of wild animals here in those days. In their first year my parents lived in a dugout. There was no door in the house. One day, my mother turned around and saw a baby bear just standing in the doorway. She didn't have time to be afraid. She just picked up a spade and hit him on the head. She killed him just like that.

The woman on the homestead worked no less strenuously than did her husband on the railroad or in the mine. In the absence of the man, the burden of tilling the land fell onto her shoulders. During the months of mild weather, the woman picked up the axe, grubhoe and spade and headed for the bush. Whatever work her husband had begun before he left, she now continued with the help of their older children. She brushed the land, dug the new soil, seeded the small crop and harvested it. She snared game for her family, walked great distances to get supplies, even put up buildings by herself.

Victoria Zaharia   When I was fourteen, I came to Canada with my father and stepmother. My father put up the walls for a house. Then he went to find work. So my stepmother and I had to finish the house. My stepmother took the scythe, went to the slough and cut the grass. I carried it in bundles on my shoulder back to the house. We put the grass on the house for a roof. Still there was no door, no windows. We huddled together in the dry corners when it rained. Then we called a neighbour who helped us put in doors and windows. Later we dug clay, mixed it with straw and plastered the house. Still my father was away. We brushed the land, burned the wood by ourselves.

Eva Kretzul   Women did everything when men were away. My mother dug land with a spade. She seeded the crops, cut them with a sickle in the fall. She stooked them and bundled them. Then she ground flour with a hand mill. Later, when there was a big mill in Lamont, she would take the wheat there. She and another woman would go together by sleigh. It took them three days.

One spring, she built a house all by herself. She cut logs, did everything. The only help she got was putting in the doors and windows. Later that summer she had her ninth child.

When my father finally sent enough money to buy a cow, my mother walked to get it. She took two of the kids with her. She walked all the way to Lamont and back again with those two kids, about forty miles.

The pioneer woman's work didn't end with the heavy homestead chores. She also had to attend to more traditional women's work: keeping her family clean, fed, and clothed.

Ukrainian women on a homestead near Theodore, Saskatchewan.

There were no modern conveniences to lighten her load. Everything had to be done the hard way, by hand. Before she could even begin to feed her family, she had to find some way of cooking. Eventually, she would build herself a clay oven, but at first she often had to resort to more primitive methods.

Victoria Zaharia   My stepmother found an old piece of pipe, flattened it out, set it over a fire and cooked on it outside, like an Indian. We cooked that way for a long time.

It wasn't always easy to put together a meal from the scant provisions she had on hand. On many occasions she would go hungry herself to allow her children to have a little more.

Keeping the dugout clean was a housewife's nightmare. She could sweep it countless times with her home-made willow broom, and still dirt and dust were everywhere. When it rained hard, the house turned into one huge mudhole. There was nothing to be done, but wait for it to dry.

Washing the family's clothes was a long and heavy chore. First the woman soaked her laundry overnight in a barrel of water that had been strained through poplar ashes. The ashes served as a cheap substitute for the soap she could not afford. The following morning, she loaded the clothes onto a wagon, or onto her back, and hauled them to the nearest stream or river, where the water would be softer than the water from her well. Here she repeatedly pounded and scrubbed the clothes on a wooden washboard, then rinsed them in the water, until they were white enough to satisfy her critical eye. The clothes were then carried back home, and hung up or spread out to dry. Even in the depths of winter, the scrupulous housewife took her laundry to the river and cut a hole through the ice to wash them in the soft water below.

Bill Shandro I remember how the women would take their clothes to wash in the river in winter. The bottoms of their skirts would get wet and freeze right up. They stood out stiff, just like boards.

Late in the evening, when no outside work could be done, the pioneer woman sat for hours by a dim light, mending and re-mending her family's well-worn clothing.

Building a House

The first tangible reward for the pioneer family's long period of privation and hard work came when they built their first comfortable home. The day construction began was a joyous and memorable occasion. It marked the immigrants' first step towards the better life for which they had come to Canada.

Like all recent immigrants, the Ukrainians carried on in the new country the traditions they had learned in the old. Within a few short years of their arrival, the picturesque Ukrainian village house, with its neat plastered and whitewashed walls and its high thatched roof became a common feature of the western prairie landscape.

Construction began with the laying of foundation stones on the location where the house was to stand. Wood was a plentiful commodity on the homestead, and logs for housebuilding were usually cut on the spot. But people who wanted wood of the best quality sometimes chose to haul it over long distances.

Pioneer house at Wostok, Alberta, 1902.

George Miskey   I spent a winter in a log shack with a young couple who were just building a bigger house. The man was cutting timber about fifteen miles away from home. We would go into the bush with oxen to haul it back. This was very slow work. We could only take three logs at a time, and a round trip took twenty-four hours. It took us several weeks to haul all the lumber.

With saws and axes, the family trimmed logs to the required lengths, stripped them, and cut grooves into the ends. Then, by laying the logs so that each one fit into the grooves of the ones beneath it, they built up the four outer and two inner walls of the house. Nails were rarely used; instead, the pioneers strengthened the walls by drilling holes through the logs, and fitting them with wooden pegs.

Openings for a door and a few small windows were cut in the walls, and fitted with frames. Glass window panes had to be purchased in town. The door could be fashioned on the spot by nailing together several thick planks with cross pieces of wood. Initially the family would have to content itself with a dirt floor; later a wooden floor would be laid down.

Some houses were built with shingle roofs, but more common in the first years was the thatched roof, made of slough grass or rye straw tied in bundles to a wooden roof frame. The roof on the Ukrainian settler's house was always very steep, with a rise of about

Details of house construction: a corner of a house. Each log fits neatly into the groove cut into the log beneath it.

nine inches to the foot. The chimney was built of bricks or stone. Some settlers built no chimney at all; they simply left the smoke to seep out through the straw roof of the house.

With the completion of the roof, the heaviest house-building work was finished. All that remained now was to finish off the rough log walls. In accordance with old-country tradition, the Ukrainian settlers plastered their house walls with a mixture of clay, straw, horse manure and water, which was trampled with the feet until it reached the proper sticky consistency. With this plaster, they filled all

Roof-thatching.

chinks between the logs, and covered the walls, inside and out, with a smooth surface coating. After the walls were completely dry, a layer of finer plaster, composed of clay and horse manure only, was applied. Then a coat of whitewash − and the house was ready for occupancy.

Most pioneer families built their own houses, each member sharing in the labour according to his strength and ability. Sometimes, a neighbour skilled in carpentry was called in for the more complicated jobs of installing doors and windows. He would rarely be paid for his labour in cash. Instead, he might be offered homemade goods or farm produce, or promised a return favour sometime in the future.

Tom Predy I was a good carpenter so I did some building for another farmer nearby. The man had no money to pay me. Money was so scarce at that time. So he paid me with a few sacks of oats for my horses.

When the happy family finally made its move into the new house, the old dugout was relegated to the status of chicken coop or storage place. They now had a shelter that was solid and comfortable, a place they could really call a home. The thick plastered walls of the new house retained heat in winter and kept it out in summer. With its

A family in front of their house near Vegreville, about 1909.

steep roof that allowed rain and snow to run down easily, it was far more waterproof than the sod roof dugout had been.

On the inside, virtually every settler's house followed the same pattern, the pattern that had been laid down by centuries of tradition. The house always faced south; it had three rooms; the room on the west side was always the kitchen. Because it was the centre of family activity, this was the largest room. One of the kitchen walls was taken up with a big clay oven that had space for baking, a metal plate for cooking, and a large flat top that served at night as a warm bed for the small children. Like the walls, the oven was whitewashed, and sometimes even decorated with colourful designs. At least once a year, at Easter, it would be refurbished with a fresh coat of white wash.

The room on the east side served as a living room and a bedroom for the older members of the family. On one of the walls were hung ikons, or holy pictures, framed with hand-embroidered cloth.

Between the two main rooms was a central hallway, which was used as an all-purpose storage space. On occasion, it even served as a temporary shelter for the family's sheep or chickens, until a separate shed could be built to house them.

Every house had a deep root cellar in which fresh food was kept cool in summer and produce stored over the winter.

An indoor clay oven built by a woman in Alberta about 1905. The metal plate (right) served as a tove for cooking. The oven (opening on the left) was sed for baking. The warm, lat top of the oven made a comfortable bed.

Furnishing was sparse. There might be a wooden table, a few homemade benches that were used as seats by day and beds by night, and the large wooden chests in which the immigrants had brought their belongings. For decoration, colourful home-woven tapestries were hung on the walls.

The pioneer home was humble, but it was a vast improvement over the dingy dugout in which the family had weathered its first years on the homestead. Here there was room for the family to live and grow for many years to come.

3 Living on the Land

Most Ukrainian immigrants were penniless. They were uneducated. But they were far from helpless. They came with a rich resource of traditional skills that were invaluable for survival on the Canadian homestead.

The life of the peasants in Ukrainian villages was ruled by tradition, not only in matters of religion and social custom, but also in practical day-to-day activities. Where formal education was lacking, tradition stepped in to fill the gap. Tradition told the peasants how to build their houses out of wood, clay and straw. Tradition told them how to work their tiny plots of land most productively. Tradition taught illiterate women to be accomplished artists capable of creating out of hemp, flax and wool, clothing and blankets of exquisite workmanship.

Their fund of traditional lore enabled the village people to be self-sufficient. They could fill all their basic needs without money and without recourse to urban markets and manufactured goods. Village traditions remained essentially unchanged for centuries. They were passed down through the generations, from father to son, from mother to daughter.

This was the background from which the Ukrainian immigrants emerged. The turn-of-the-century western Canada to which they flocked was an undeveloped land. There were no large cities and no factories churning out goods. There were no transportation links between the remote homesteads and market towns. And there was

no immediate possibility of earning enough money to buy even the supplies that were available. But unlike some of the other new settlers, who had always been used to the amenities of urban life and were hard put to do without them, the Ukrainians had a life-long preparation for the rigorous lifestyle homesteading demanded. They didn't have to learn from scratch how to be self-sufficient.

On their homesteads the Ukrainians set about to recreate the way of life they had known in their native villages, in so far as was possible in a country so different from their own. Unaffected by the ways of the English-speaking people that surrounded their closely-knit little colonies, the immigrants continued to do as they had always done. Ukrainian village houses appeared in the bushlands of Alberta, Saskatchewan and Manitoba. Out of new-country materials the settlers fashioned their old-country tools of survival: flour mills, oil presses, clay ovens, looms and simple farm tools. Once established in this way, they hardly needed to rely on the world outside their communities. From the wood that surrounded them, the grain, seed crops and vegetables they grew on their cleared land, and the livestock they raised on their farms, the settlers provided their own food, their own clothing and their own shelter.

For the first twenty-five years, their traditional skills sustained the Ukrainian settlers. They enabled this most disadvantaged group of immigrants, starting in poverty in an inhospitable environment, to survive, progress and eventually prosper.

By the end of the First World War some changes were making themselves felt. Age-old customs began to give way in the face of new conditions. By dint of dedicated, ceaseless toil, each settler's land clearing progressed steadily. In time, his holdings grew too large to be worked in the traditional way. Seeders, mowers, threshers began to replace scythes and flails. The larger wheat crop could no longer be ground by hand; it was hauled to a large, efficient mill in one of the new towns that were growing up all over the prairies. Old-world village clothing that had been made so patiently by hand was being abandoned in favour of Canadian fashions. The self-contained, tradition-bound Ukrainian settlements were opening up to the influence of the society around them.

Tilling the Soil

The promise of land lured the Ukrainians to Canada, and the land claimed all their attention. Men, women and children applied themselves singlemindedly to improving the homestead, giving it precedence above all else. To clear a bit more land, to sow a little more grain, to acquire another cow or a few more chickens — this was their overriding goal. Whatever money flowed in from outside employment was channeled into the homestead, for ploughs, for work animals, for livestock. All other needs and wants were sacrificed. And slowly, neat little farms were emerging from the wilderness.

The pioneer farm was hardly larger than the meagre piece of land the immigrant family had left behind. If a man had ten acres cleared his neighbours considered him wealthy. But already there was enough grain ripening in his field to put bread on the table and to make feed for his animals. Alongside the grain, tall hemp plants, sunflowers and full-blown poppies were growing in long straight rows. Near the house, a vegetable garden flourished.

A thatch-roof barn on a farm near Teulon, Manitoba.

In the yard, the settler erected a granary and barns to house the gradually increasing animal population. The first cow, the family's original source of nourishment, now grazed side by side with others. A few hogs, chickens and a flock of sheep roamed through the yard.

Mrs. Kowalchuk At first my father ploughed with oxen. He sowed his crop by hand. He would swing a bag of seeds over his shoulder, then walk through the field and throw the seeds onto the ground. He cut hay with a scythe. He threshed his grain with a flail.

At first the pioneer farmer worked his land in Canada as his ancestors had done for countless generations before him: by hand, with tools that were mostly homemade. Only the plough and the metal blades of sickles and scythes had to be purchased. The rest of his equipment – harrows, flails, rakes, winnowers, forks, sickle and scythe handles – he fashioned himself, out of wood, leather thongs and strands of wire.

Pioneer farm costs

The cost of running a farm has skyrocketed in recent years. The price of machinery, of fuel to run it, of specially prepared animal feeds adds up to a small fortune. For the Ukrainian settler ready cash was a scarce commodity. But the capital outlay to outfit and run his farm was small. Even the poor immigrant could save enough from his outside wages to meet the basic costs at these turn-of-the-century rates:

Team of oxen $70.00
Plough $25.00
Scythe blade $1.00
Sickle Blade $1.00
Taxes* $2.00-10.00

*Varied with the location of the homestead and the amount of land cleared.

A settler breaks a recently-cleared field near Lloydminster, Alberta-Saskatchewan boundary, about 1900. In spring, he broke his few acres of cleared land with a walking plough. A pair of oxen pulled it while the man walked behind, steering it evenly through the soil. He went over the land once more, with a wooden harrow, then walked through the furrows broadcasting his seeds.

Good Years . . . And Bad

Farm Tools

The sickle was the tool of the harvest. When the grain was ripe, the settler cut it with a sickle. As he worked, he bundled the grain and tied it into sheaves with its own straw.

Flails were pioneer threshers. Late in the fall or in winter, after the harvested grain was well dried, it was laid out on the floor of the barn or a sheet of ice. Husband and wife, or father and son, each one armed with a flail, stood facing each other and beat the grain hard in rhythm until the grain was separated from the straw. To clean the threshed grain, the settlers winnowed it. The best time *continued*

The Good Life, whose image had beckoned to the downtrodden Ukrainian peasant from posters advertising Canadian homesteads was coming ever closer to reality. The promised prosperity wasn't his yet, but already the grim daily battle with cold and near-starvation was a thing of the past. Each year brought the immigrant family a more abundant harvest, a little more money in hand, a brighter prospect for the future. On warm summer evenings, the home-steader could stroll through his little fields, see a fine crop growing up, and dream of the day when the whole of his quarter section would be transformed into rippling fields of wheat.

The rate of progress on the homestead varied from family to family, from region to region. Those who came with more money, those who earned it more quickly after they arrived, those who settled on clearer land and more fertile soil had a better head start than their less fortunate compatriots.

But whatever the individual rate of progress might have been, the growth on each homestead was making a dramatic change in the overall picture of the Canadian West. Agricultural production was increasing significantly year by year. To consider Manitoba alone: in 1881 there were 51,300 acres under cultivation in the province. By 1902, after a massive influx of immigrants from many lands, there were 3,189,000. In 1880 Manitoba produced 5 million bushels of wheat; in 1905 it produced 55 million bushels. The presence of thousands of settlers scattered across the West, each one working patiently on his small patch of land, was making itself felt in a big way.

Farm Tools *continued*
for winnowing was a windy day. The settlers swept their grain kernels into a wooden basin, held the basin high in the air, then tipped the kernels out slowly. The heavy grain fell to the ground, while the lighter chaff blew away in the wind. For a final cleaning, the grain was sifted through a sieve with holes just large enough to let the grain fall through, but not the chaff.

(far left)
Home-made wooden forks were useful for a wide variety of farm chores.
(near left)
Wheat sheaf, flail, sickle, winnower.
(bottom left)
Team of oxen on a Teulon, Manitoba farm.
Oxen provided all the power on the pioneer farm. These ungainly beasts were slower than horses, but they were cheaper to buy, and being less fussy eaters, more economical to feed.
The oxen served their owners well. Hitched to a plough or harrow, they helped the settler work his land, then doubled as a means of transportation, pulling a wagon in summer and a sleigh in winter.
(right)
Ukrainian homesteaders rejoice at a good harvest.

But there were breaks in the line of progress. With only a precarious footing in the new country, the settlers were still highly vulnerable to forces beyond their control: general economic trends and the whims of nature. They had no reserves of cash salted away for a rainy day. There was no crop insurance, no accident insurance, no welfare scheme. If a sudden fire swept through a settler's house and barns, razing them to the ground; if the unpredictable prairie weather brought drought, hail or frost that destroyed his crops — there was nothing he could do but stand by stoically and watch several years of hard work slip away to nothing.

Victoria Zaharia   During the years my husband was out working we had some bad years of frost. All the wheat froze, and the flour was terrible. I remember we used to say about the bread we made that it was only good for plastering houses. But we had to eat it. It was all we had.

Tom Predy   1914-1918 were depression years. Nobody had any money. We killed rabbits, kept a few chickens. We had a garden but all we could grow was potatoes. The frost was so bad even in summer that other vegetables wouldn't grow. Once during this time I killed a big coyote. I took the skin into town and sold it for $16.00. That seemed like so much money! I felt like a rich man. It was just before Christmas, so I went and bought some nice food for the family.

Victoria Zaharia   We didn't have a henhouse, so we kept our chickens in a hole in the ground, with a roof over it and the chinks filled with hay. One day I went with my father to press oil. While I was away, my husband put some hay in the henhouse, but he put too much. When I came back, all the chickens were dead — suffocated. I was so sorry. We had to go the rest of the summer without any chickens. We couldn't afford to buy new ones right away.

Food Production

If a Ukrainian peasant dropped a piece of bread onto the ground, he picked it up and kissed it contritely. Bread was sacred; to waste food was an unpardonable sin. Waste was unknown on the pioneer farm. The thrifty settlers made efficient use of every product of the land.

The family's daily fare was plain and wholesome: bread, fresh or smoked meat, borshch (beet soup), holubtsi (cabbage rolls), pyrohy (dumplings) filled with potatoes or sauerkraut and dairy products. A sweet cake, a fresh apple or orange were treats rare enough to turn a child's eyes wide with delight. But so long as the land was productive, so long as the livestock grew sleek and contented, there was no danger of going hungry.

The farmwife tended her garden with an almost religious zeal. All summer long she was rewarded for her care with crisp green vegetables for her table. As the season drew to a close, she worked feverishly to preserve her crop for the coming winter. Masses of cabbage were shredded, made into sauerkraut and stored away in enormous 45-gallon barrels. Some cabbage leaves were left whole to be used later for cabbage rolls. Potatoes, onions and carrots were piled high in the root cellar.

(left)
Butter churn.
(centre)
This mill was built in 1905.
To grind flour, the settler
fed his wheat into the hole
in the centre of the top
stone. While he turned the
top stone, the bottom one
remained stationary.
Between these two stones,
the wheat was crushed,
and came pouring out as
flour from the hole in the
side of the mill.
Every so often, as the
stones wore smooth
through constant use, they
were roughened again with
hammers and chisels.
(right)
This huge contraption is an
oil press, a roughly hewn
version of an old country
machine. This one was
built in Alberta in 1895.
The machine is made
entirely of wood. One such
press in a district kept the
whole population well
supplied with vegetable oil.

The cow provided abundant supplies of milk, cheese, sweet cream and the sour cream the settlers loved to pour generously over their pyrohy and stir into their borshch. The daily chores of milking the cow and churning cream into butter fell to the children by turn. Each day their mother sent them out to collect eggs from the henhouse. On special occasions, she killed a chicken to serve for the family dinner.

Fresh meat wouldn't keep for long without refrigeration. The traditional practice of smoking meat enabled the settlers to preserve it safely. Once or twice a year hogs were butchered, and the meat was turned into tasty hams and a variety of sausages. The high ceiling of the Ukrainian house was ideally designed for smoking meat. Hams and sausages were suspended from the rafters, and there they hung for several weeks, curing in the smoke that drifted upwards as wood burned in the stove.

Even inedible parts of the butchered animal were put to good use. From the lining of the hog's stomach came rennet, a basic ingredient for making cheese. The membrane was cut into small pieces, dried and salted, then put into milk to begin the curdling process that eventually produced cheese. The hog's intestines made a natural casing for sausage meat.

To preserve mushrooms, berries and fish the settlers dried them. The food was laid out in the sun for several days, or heated slowly in the oven.

A product commonly made at home was "moonshine." Homemade drink was cheaper and, the settlers believed, far superior to the store-bought variety. Private stills turning out a potent beverage from potatoes, rye, or whatever else the distiller had on hand, proliferated underground and in other secret places hidden well away from the prying eyes of the RCMP. At weddings and festive occasions the moonshine flowed freely, but it was highly regarded for its medicinal properties as well. The settlers could not depend on professional care in times of illness. The nearest doctor could well be a hundred miles away, and even if he could be reached, chances were he wouldn't know a word of Ukrainian. So home remedies were the order of the day. Innumerable asthma attacks or bouts of the flu were sent on their way with a stiff shot of moonshine.

Daily Bread

When immigration officer C. W. Speers visited the Edna/Star colony in Alberta, he found the settlers already busily milling their small wheat crops into flour. He described how they went about it in the following letter to his superior:

Kaye, p. 348. *They have in two places small mills in the colony made by themselves — one operated by two horses on a stationary power, with rope belting turning two large stones that have been chiselled and fitted to grind with a small agitating hopper suspended above. . . . At another place I saw a small mill in the house that would grind two bushels of wheat per day; a woman working it by hand — verily "a woman grinding at the mill."*

To Mr. Speers, the sight of a woman grinding wheat by hand was quaint and un-Canadian — he called it an "Oriental habit," and hoped it would "soon pass away." But he conceded that this practice enabled the Ukrainian immigrants, "by their industry and ingenuity to save a long haul of thirty miles to the Grist Mill."

The means with which to grind flour for their daily bread was important to the Ukrainians, so important that some immigrants hauled millstones with them half-way around the world. Almost every family had its own mill. Those who didn't took their wheat to a neighbouring homestead. After a full day of turning his neighbour's mill, a settler could return home with a full sack of flour slung over his shoulder.

Pressing Oil

Every family kept on hand several gallon-sized jugs of cooking oil extracted from the seeds of home-grown hemp, poppies and sunflowers. The Ukrainians used oil liberally: they cooked with it and put large quantities into their sauerkraut. During periods of fast, which came frequently for these religious people, oil served as a substitute for animal fats and dairy products, all of which were forbidden foods.

Oil pressing wasn't done at home. Extensive equipment was required for the job, and there was no need for every family to have its own. In any given area of Ukrainian settlement, one person took on the responsibility of building and operating an oil press. The rest of the settlers took their seeds to him, to be pressed for a small monetary fee or payment in goods.

At peak oil pressing time — in the fall after the harvest and early in spring before the start of the long Easter Lent — the machinery was kept going around the clock. Settlers streamed to the press owner's homestead from all around in wagons loaded up with sacks full of seeds. With such a great demand for the pressman's services, a family might have to wait two or three days for its turn at the press. But the customers didn't mind the wait. It gave them an opportunity to socialize with their neighbours. They pitched camp in the pressman's yard, and whiled away the hours in merry conversation. Invariably someone pulled out a bottle of moonshine. People caught up with the latest gossip, and sat up late into the night telling jokes, singing, discussing the harvest and reminiscing about their homeland.

The man who owned the oil press built a one-room shack to house his equipment. Inside he had a seed crusher, a large wooden press and a tin stove. As each customer brought in his seeds, the pressman put them through the crusher, then mixed the crushed seeds with warm water. He heated this mixture on the stove, wrapped it in a thick woollen cloth and set it on the press, directly under the central cylinder. Operating the press was a heavy job that took the strength of two burly men. The pressman and his assistant took their places on each side of the press and swung around the two large hammers. The hammers pushed in wedges on top of the cylinder, driving it down onto the seeds with a force of several tons. The pressure squeezed out the oil, which came running out of a hole in the press into buckets waiting below. After each operation of the press, a flat cake of seed husks remained. These cakes the customer took back home. Most often he fed them to the pigs, but they could be mixed with water and cooked into a porridge for the children.

The enterprising pressman sometimes made a point of "forgetting" to return these cakes to his customers. When he accumulated a large number, he put them through the press once more, and thus got a gallon or two of free oil for himself.

The Ukrainians so loved their home produced hemp and poppy oil that they continued to press it for years, even after commercially made oil was readily available. It wasn't until 1949, when the RCMP forbade farmers to grow the potentially narcotic hemp and poppy plants, that community oil presses ceased to operate.

Cooking the Meals

Out in the yard near the settlers' house stood a capacious outdoor clay oven in which the farmwife did most of her cooking.

Each woman built her own oven, out of wood, clay and stones. She began by erecting a wooden platform, which she covered with a layer of stones. Over this base she bent thick willow branches into a semi-circular shape, and wove finer branches through them to make a sturdy frame. The frame and the stone base she covered with a thick coat of plaster made up of clay, horse manure and sand. Within a few days, when the plaster was dry, the oven was ready for use.

A well constructed oven would stand for years, as long as minor repairs were carried out regularly. Once a year a new layer of plaster was slapped onto the outside of the oven to replace what had been washed away by the rain. From time to time the interior had to be refurbished. This job most often fell to one of the small children who could crawl into the oven with no trouble, and sit comfortably inside while smoothing on a coat of freshly-mixed plaster.

To prepare her oven for baking, the woman filled it with dry willow and spruce boughs, lit them, and allowed them to burn for an hour or more. She had no thermometer, but she had her own ways of testing the oven temperature. An experienced cook needed do no more than place her hand in the oven opening; by the feel of the heat she could judge instantly whether the oven was ready. Alternatively, she might throw a handful of flour in to see how quickly it scorched, or scratch the oven bottom with a metal tool: a hot oven produced a large spark.

When she was satisfied that the temperature was just right, the woman raked out the remains of the fire, put her food into the oven and closed the front opening with a wooden door. If she was preparing a large meal that required several hours of cooking, she

Even today some women continue to bake in outdoor clay ovens. The ovens are particularly useful for preparing large quantities of food on special occasions – or for baking enough bread to feed a large farm family.

The dough is rolled out and braided into twist loaves.

The fire is lit and left to burn for an hour, heating up the oven.

Then the ashes are raked
out.

The pans of bread are
pushed inside.

A wooden door seals the oven, holding in the heat, while the bread bakes.

After an hour, the loaves are taken out.

sealed the gap around the door and the rear ventilation hole with fresh clay. This way, no heat could escape.

Store bought metal baking dishes were sometimes beyond the means of the immigrant farmwife, but she wasn't at a loss to make her own. When baking pyrohy or twist loaves of bread, she cut a few large cabbage leaves in her garden, laid the food on them and slid them into the oven. The leaves not only worked well as dishes; they even enhanced the flavour of the food.

During the summer months the outdoor oven was constantly on the go; there was no need for the woman to overheat her house by cooking indoors. But even in winter, on occasions that called for large quantities of food, she fired up her outside oven and carried dishes of food out through the snow.

Clothing

The Ukrainians stood out sharply in the crowds of people who streamed from immigrant boats and trains into Canadian cities. In contrast to the sombre suits and plain dresses of Western Europeans, the costumes of Ukrainians branded them immediately as an exotic breed of foreigner. The men in bleached linen homespuns and thick sheepskin coats, the women in profusely embroidered shirts, their heads wrapped in colourful shawls and waists cinched with belts woven in geometric patterns, couldn't fail to make an impression — not always favourable — on the people who watched the immigrants disembark.

In the Ukrainian village, each woman made her family's clothing, household linen and blankets. Only the sewing of boots and sheep-skin coats was left to specialists. By observing and helping her mother, every peasant girl learned from early childhood the skills needed to turn hemp, flax and wool into cloth. She learned through painful practice how to spin the rough, sharp hemp fibres into a strong thread, then how to weave it into cloth and embroider it according to traditional designs, which varied from province to province, and even from village to village. In the Ukrainian woman's handiwork, artistry and practicality met. The goods she produced were both beautiful and extremely durable. A woollen tapestry or a hemp shirt lasted not for years, but for generations, and was commonly passed down, still in good condition, from mother to daughter to granddaughter.

Distaffs and spindles, wool and hemp carders were among the essential items the Ukrainian woman packed into her trunk as she prepared to leave for Canada. Often she packed away some hemp

Costumes like this one had been worn for centuries by the women of Bukovina. Ukrainian immigrant women arrived in Canada in these clothes, and continued to wear them in the new country. Except for the kerchief, every part of this costume was made by hand. The woollen skirt and belt were woven in Ukraine, in the village of Toporiwtsi. They were brought to Alberta in an immigrant's trunk in 1910. The shirt was made of hemp on a Canadian homestead.

seeds as well. With these, she started a new crop on the homestead. To assure herself of a supply of wool, she either kept a small herd of white long-haired sheep, or arranged to buy wool from a neighbour. Shortly after her arrival, her husband, or a local carpenter, built her a loom, which she placed in her living room or in a separate shed near the house. Many of her evening hours were spent sitting at her loom.

Hemp Of all the crops grown on the homestead, hemp was the most versatile. Its seeds gave the settlers cooking oil; from its stems came the fibre for their cloth.

(left)
Hemp crusher and loose fibres: The woman pulled each hemp stem slowly across the crusher, systematically beating it with the side board as she pulled.

(right)
Hemp carder: The teeth on this carder are made of large nails. It took a hefty carder to comb out the thick hemp fibres. The carder was attached firmly to a bench, and the fibres pulled through it several times.

In fall, each woman pulled up her ripe hemp plants. To soften the stems, she soaked them in the water of a nearby creek or stream for several days, then laid them out on the bank to dry in the sun. A week or two later, she pounded the dry stems vigorously on a hemp crusher until all the fibres were loosened. To clean the fibres thoroughly of all waste material, the woman pulled them repeatedly through a long-spiked hemp carder. Finally the hemp was ready to be spun into thread.

There was no spinning wheel on the homestead. The Ukrainian woman worked her thread in a simpler and more ancient way, with a distaff and spindle. She fixed the distaff to a bench or table so that it remained stationary; on it she tied her carded hemp — or wool — in a neat bundle. With the smooth, measured motion of one hand, she pulled out the fibres; with the other hand she twirled them quickly and skillfully onto the spindle, twisting them into an even thread.

Even the most experienced spinner couldn't make thread as quickly by hand as on a wheel, but the old-fashioned spinning method had its advantage: it was completely portable. Wherever the woman went, her spinning went with her. When she paused for a rest from her heavy outdoor chores, she picked up her spinning and

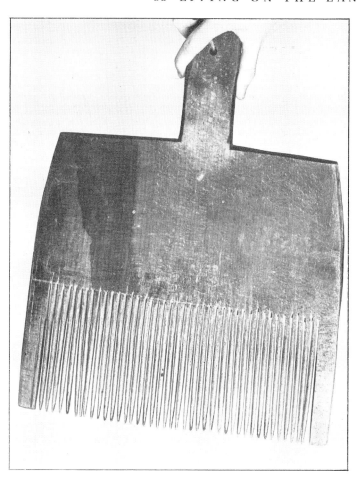

(left)
A wool carder, well over one hundred years old. It was used in the village of Ruskiy-Banyliw in Bukovina for many years before it was brought to Canada in 1899.

(right)
Spinning wool: Fluffy white wool, freshly washed and carded, is tied in a neat bundle to the distaff. With the spindle it is twisted into thread.

turned out a few more yards of thread. On long, dark winter nights she spun in the house by the fire. On warm afternoons, she sat in the sun on a bench beside the house, spinning while she kept a watchful eye on her small children at play. Even when visiting she took her spinning with her and worked busily with her hands as she chatted with her neighbours.

From the thread that she spun so diligently, she wove cloth on her loom. No fine or delicate garments would be made from hemp. The cloth was rough and very strong, ideally suited for the everyday clothes of hardworking farmers.

Shirts and household linen were always white, decorated with multi-coloured embroidery. To whiten her cloth, the woman soaked it thoroughly and spread it on the ground to be dried and bleached by the sun. Then she cut out her garments, embroidered them on the sleeves and around the neck, and sewed them together.

Wool Skirts, belts, thick warm blankets and decorative tapestries were made out of wool. In spring, the sheep were sheared of their thick

(above)
An old prune box turned into a machine for winding thread. Each colour of thread was wound onto a different bobbin. While weaving a tapestry on her loom, the woman changed colours as the pattern required.
(above right)
A hand-built loom like this one sat in almost every pioneer house. On it the woman wove her hemp threads into a sturdy cloth, and wool into rugs and tapestries.
(right)
Traditional Ukrainian clothing, all spun, woven, embroidered and sewn by hand.
(opposite top left)
Elaborately embroidered cushion.
(opposite top right)
Tapestry woven out of wool thread in a colourful traditional design.

(lower left)
Old men passed their leisure hours weaving hats out of wheat straw. The straw was cut when it was most pliable, before it was fully ripe. This old-country-style hat was woven by an Alberta settler when he was in his eighties.
(lower right)
Multi-coloured hand-woven belts were worn by men and women alike.

winter coats. The raw wool was washed thoroughly to remove its natural grease, carded, tied in a fluffy bunch to the distaff, and spun into thread in the same way as the hemp fibres. Unlike hemp cloth, most woollen goods were brightly coloured. When she finished spinning her wool thread, the woman wound it into skeins and dyed each skein in a different colour – red, green, orange, yellow, black. At one time, all dyes were made at home from natural sources. Some colours came from the leaves of plants; others came from flowers, tree bark and the skins of onions. But in Canada, where factory-made dyes were easily available, few women took the time to make their own.

When all the thread was dyed, the woman wove it into belts, blankets and tapestries, always following a traditional pattern.

Mrs. Homeniuk At first I always wore my Ukrainian clothes. After I got married, while we still lived with my parents, I still wore them. But when my husband and I moved away, I stopped wearing them except for Sundays. The younger people were changing to Canadian clothes and my husband didn't want me to wear the old style clothes any more. He wanted me to dress in style.

Of all the traditional women's crafts, the production of hemp clothing had the shortest life on Canadian soil. In part, this was because a wide variety of manufactured cloth was sold in every small town general store. Store-bought cloth wasn't as strong as the home made, but it was cheap, and it spared the woman many hours of painstaking labour. But even more important was the growing pressure on the Ukrainians to conform to the norms of the society outside their small communities. Having gone to schools and into towns, having seen that other Canadians didn't dress in homespuns, the younger people began to abandon these obvious marks of their ''foreignness'' in favour of more fashionable apparel. By 1918 most young women were making the change to Canadian dresses and skirts for everyday wear; their long hemp shirts and woollen over-skirts were reserved for Sundays and holidays. Only the older women, unable to break with a deeply-ingrained tradition, clung faithfully to their old-world style of dress.

But not all the handiwork was given up so quickly. Embroidery and the weaving of woollen tapestries, which could not be replaced as readily with factory-made goods, continued to occupy the women's spare hours.

Around the Homestead

Every homesteader had to be his own carpenter and handyman. With a few basic tools he made for himself almost everything he needed for his home and his farm. To save himself the long trip into town, he braided his own rope from hemp. He made yokes for his teams of oxen and feeding troughs for his pigs. Out of willow branches he wove neat, strong fences. From the wood on his homestead he fashioned furniture for his house and a variety of useful odds and ends.

(top left)
Hollowing tool: With this tool the settler hollowed bowls and troughs out of solid pieces of wood.

(top right)
The troughs had a variety of uses. Large ones were used to hold feed for his hogs. Smaller ones served as mixing bowls in which his wife kneaded dough for her bread. They even found a use as baby cradles.

(centre)
A mouse wouldn't stand much of a chance if it was tempted by the food that baited this home-made mousetrap. The bait was tied with a string to the piece of wood holding up the top of the trap. As the mouse nibbled on the bait, it pulled the string, and the top came crashing down.

Home-made plane.

4 Family, Social and Religious Life

As they stepped from immigrant ships onto Canadian shores, the Ukrainians were sealing their future. For all but a small minority, emigration was a permanent undertaking. Canada was forever to be their home.

So they had to make it feel like home. Converting their quarter sections of bush into habitable and productive land was the most urgent, but not the only step in the complex process of building a new life in a new country. Emigration involved far more than just abandoning an old piece of land for a new one. It meant severing long-standing family and social ties. It meant leaving far behind the cultural and religious institutions and the whole network of customs and traditions that formed the basis of village life.

Scattered across the gaping emptiness of the Canadian West, the settlers felt lost, uprooted, homeless. Individually and collectively, they would have to take up the loose strands of their lives and weave them once again into a stable pattern. The initial phase of Ukrainian settlement in Canada was a period of transition, adjustment and development. On the one hand, the settlers strove to re-establish those customs and institutions that were an integral part of their old-world lifestyle; on the other, they began gradually to accommodate themselves to the social structures of the new world.

The sense of "being at home" didn't come overnight. Poverty, discouragement and loneliness hung over every immigrant family during its first years on the homestead. Numerous obstacles, both internal and external, hindered the settlers' group efforts to establish themselves firmly on Canadian soil. Ukrainian religious life had a painful birth in Canada, marred by bitter internecine conflicts. Disunity, and misunderstanding and hostility on the part of the Anglo-Canadian population impeded the settlers' progress on the educational and political fronts.

At its inception, the community life of the Ukrainian settlers was insular: the people looked inward and backward. The Ukrainians came *en masse* into regions that had previously been uninhabited, except here and there by an English pioneer farmer, and by bands of native people who moved on to more remote regions as the tide of settlers swelled. Incoming homesteaders inevitably chose to join their countrymen. So, within a few years, enormous tracts of land in the Canadian West were settled almost exclusively by Ukrainians.

Within their homogeneous colonies, the settlers stuck together. They continued to speak their own language. They relied upon each other for help, for companionship, for entertainment. The social and religious customs of the Ukrainian village were perpetuated. At Christmas time, the settlers replayed the traditional rituals of the season, prepared the traditional Christmas Eve supper and organized carolling parties. At Easter, they decorated eggs and blessed their Easter bread. Folk ceremonies surrounding the most important events of family life — birth, marriage, death — were maintained intact. Sharing in a cohesive community life brought a sense of security to people who were living in a situation that was essentially insecure. It was an effective buffer against the shock of finding themselves in a whole new world.

But they were in a new world. Slowly they began to turn their eyes towards it. To help newcomers adjust to their new environment, numerous Ukrainian organizations and self-help groups sprang up, most of them centered in the cities where immigrants came to look for work. A significant step forward in Ukrainian *emigré* life was the appearance in western Canada of a Ukrainian language press. The *Canadian Farmer*, launched in Winnipeg in 1903, was the first of a large variety of Ukrainian newspapers that would be published throughout the prairies in the pre-war years. Immigrants who until this time relied upon old-country publications, several weeks old by the time they made their way through the international postal system, could now read, in their own language, about Canadian affairs, and gain a better understanding of the workings of their adopted country.

The first wholesale entry of Ukrainian immigrants into Canadian institutions came when children started to attend school. In most

rural colonies, a good decade slipped by before the settlers turned their attention to organizing school districts. But in time, school buildings went up, teachers were hired, and little Ukrainian boys and girls, like all other Canadian children, trotted off to school to learn reading, writing and arithmetic — in English. Limited at first, student attendance increased with each passing year. Ignorance of the new country's language was a major obstacle to the first generation of immigrants; it would no longer be so for their children.

Although a few educated and politically conscious persons were numbered in the ranks of the Ukrainian immigrants, most people had but a dim awareness of the political processes of the country they were entering. As they acquired Canadian citizenship, politicians courted their vote, but between elections they paid little heed to immigrant communities. The Ukrainians' early attempts to flex their own political muscles met with little success. They mounted a concerted campaign for the recognition of Ukrainian as a language of instruction in their schools. The political establishment, raising the spectre of Ukrainian separatism, quashed their aspirations. Ukrainians began to offer themselves as candidates in provincial and federal elections. The first to break into the closed circles of party politics was Andrew Shandro, elected as a Liberal to the Alberta Legislature in 1913. The way was opened for others to follow.

Ukrainian colonies in western Canada: The main region of Ukrainian settlement stretched in a band diagonally across the three prairie provinces, between Winnipeg and Edmonton. Typically, Ukrainian immigrants chose their homesteads along the southern edge of the parkland and forest belt. They were attracted to this hilly, wooded, well-watered region because it resembled the terrain of Galicia and Bukovina more closely than did the dry, bald prairie further south, and also because it offered them limitless supplies of firewood, a commodity that had been depleted, and was thus scarce and expensive, in their native provinces.

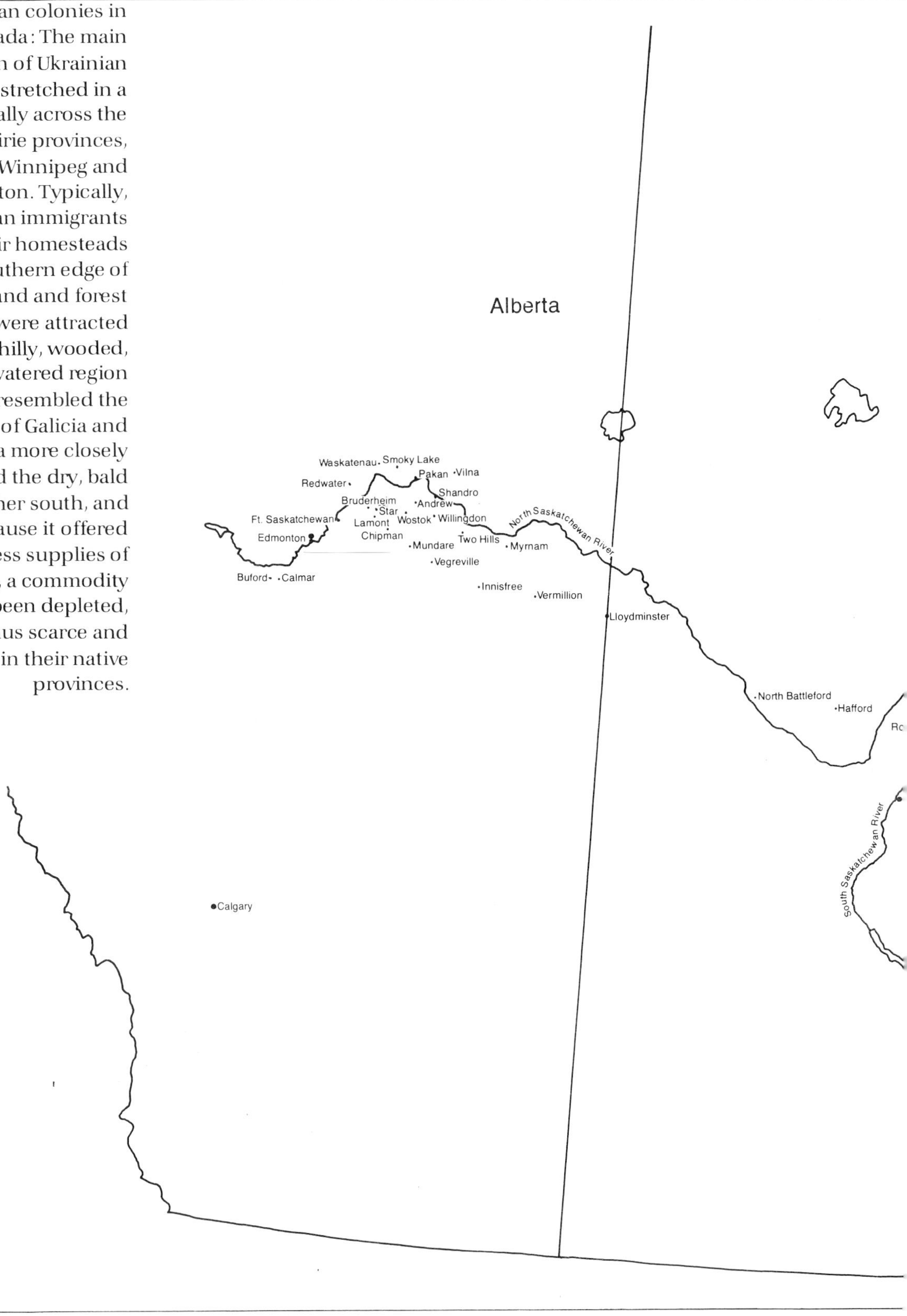

Alberta

Waskatenau· Smoky Lake
Redwater·   ·Pakan ·Vilna
         Bruderheim   ·Shandro
Ft. Saskatchewan· ·Star ·Andrew
         Lamont Wostok ·Willingdon   North Saskatchewan River
Edmonton· Chipman   ·Two Hills
                ·Mundare ·Myrnam
Buford· ·Calmar   ·Vegreville
                ·Innisfree ·Vermillion
                        ·Lloydminster

·North Battleford
        ·Hafford
            Ro

·Calgary

South Saskatchewan River

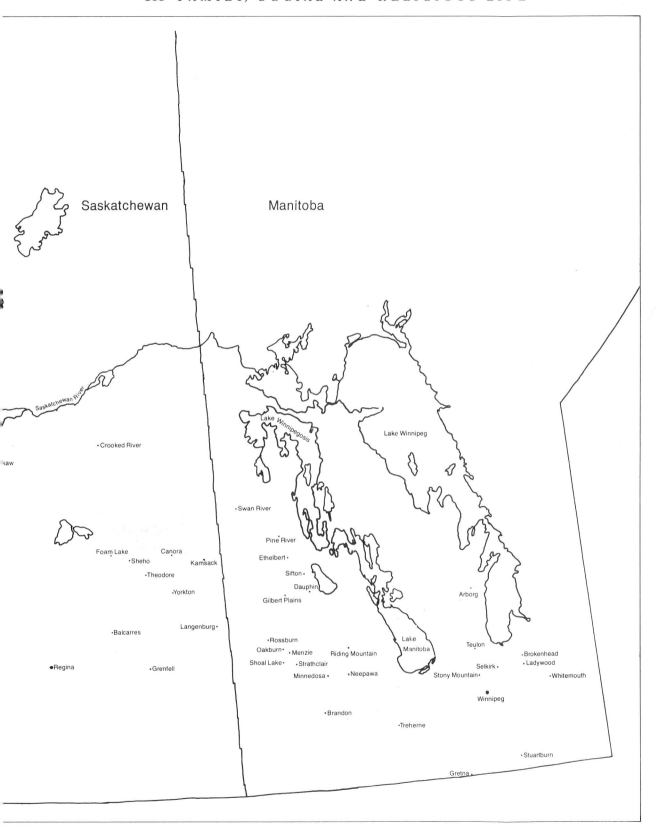

Saskatchewan

Manitoba

Saskatchewan River

Crooked River

ʘaw

Lake Winnipegosis

Lake Winnipeg

Swan River

Pine River

Foam Lake   Canora
      Sheho   Kamsack
                   Ethelbert
      Theodore
                   Sifton
              Dauphin
      Yorkton
              Gilbert Plains

Arborg

Balcarres   Langenburg

             Rossburn
      Oakburn   Menzie   Riding Mountain
Shoal Lake   Strathclair
Regina   Grenfell   Minnedosa   Neepawa

Lake Manitoba

Teulon

Brokenhead
Ladywood

Selkirk
Stony Mountain   Whitemouth

Winnipeg

Brandon

Treherne

Stuartburn

Gretna

Twenty-five years had gone by since the first contingent of Ukrainians took up residence at Star, Alberta. It was a quarter century spent in struggle. The settlers battled physical, social and psychological obstacles to create for themselves a new life on unfamiliar soil. And they were winning. The land was beginning to reward them for their patient and tireless work. Churches and schools were going up in their communities. In a small way, their voices were making themselves heard in the political spheres of the nation. By no means were the Ukrainian immigrants fully at home and at ease in their country of adoption — many of the older people never would be. But the stage was set for future generations to step forward.

The Family Hearth

Most Ukrainian immigrants came to Canada in family groups: couples, often with young children in tow, sometimes accompanied by brothers, sisters and parents. Throughout the upheaval of emigration, the duress of the early years on the homestead, the adjustment to living in a foreign land, the family unit remained intact. It provided the settlers with a stable and secure centre in a world filled with uncertainty.

Having left most of their relatives thousands of miles behind them, the immigrants began gradually to put down new family roots in their adopted country. The process of building a new life in Canada took a period of fifteen or twenty years. In that time, the family was constantly growing and changing. New children were being born on Canadian soil. People who came in their middle age were growing old. Older children who emigrated with their parents were growing up, marrying, leaving home and having children of their own. The network of family bonds and relationships, that intangible human factor that turns a mere piece of foreign land into a home in the true sense of the word, was spreading outward.

The pioneer house sheltered a large number of people under its roof. Families numbering fewer than five or six children were rare. More commonly, ten, twelve, or even more youngsters were crowded together, sleeping three or four to a bed, tucked away on top of the oven and in various corners of the two rooms. Frequently the family ranks were enlarged by the presence of unmarried aunts, uncles, cousins or aging grandparents, for relatives were always welcomed into the home. To accommodate them not only fulfilled a sacred family obligation, but served a practical purpose at the same time. Every extra mouth to feed also meant an extra pair of hands, and in that pre-mechanized era, an extra pair of hands was always useful.

In its new Canadian setting, life within the family continued to follow the traditional, old-country pattern. Relations of parents to children were stern, authoritarian, yet at the same time, affectionate. There was a set place for everyone, and everyone knew his place. Children weren't indulged. Supplies of money were far too tight to allow a child's whim for toys or new clothes to be satisfied; he had to make do with homemade playthings and well-worn hand-me-downs. But there was very little neglect of children. Surrounded as they were by so many watchful adults and older brothers and sisters, the youngest members of the family were guaranteed good care.

To keep the homestead running smoothly, all family members had to pull their weight. Husband and wife laboured side by side clearing away bush, ploughing, seeding and harvesting. Older children, both boys and girls, were recruited to help in even the heaviest chores.

Anastasia Zazula   As a young girl I worked out in the fields with horses. When I was twelve I used to help my father haul grain to the railroad in Vegreville, thirty-five miles from our farm. Until I was fifteen and got married, I helped in all the work around the farm.

Every child old enough to be entrusted with a small task was expected to help lighten the load of the overworked parents. Small children milked cows, picked roots, weeded the garden. Youngsters of seven or eight kept a sharp eye on those of two or three, while their mother busied herself in the fields or in the kitchen.

Grandparents who were too old and feeble for heavy outdoor work still had a valuable role to play in the family, taking over numerous less strenuous jobs, whether it was working in the garden, feeding the chickens, or, on the part of the women, cooking, spinning, weaving and embroidering. With many more leisure hours at their disposal than the harassed parents, the grandparents could always find the time to take youngsters onto their knees and entertain them with stories, songs and reminiscences.

The weekday routine offered little respite from work. Each day brought a succession of chores that kept the homesteaders occupied from sunrise to sunset, and left almost no time for adults to rest and children to play. But when Sunday came around, all but the most essential work ceased. On this day the children were free to run about the farm, amusing themselves with simple, improvised games and playing with homemade toys — balls made out of rags and twine, dolls pieced together from scraps of wood and cloth. On this day too,

the family could gather together for rest, relaxation — and instruction.

Anastasia Zazula My mother never went to school. But she taught all the children to say their prayers. On Sundays and holidays, when no one worked, parents would sit with their children and teach them what they needed to know.

(left)
Ukrainian immigrants in their later years. After a long lifetime of incessant work, old people could count on a place in the homes of their children and grandchildren.

(right)
Grieving family members hold a tiny coffin at a baby's funeral.

However unlettered the parents might have been, they strove to instill in their children a basic sense of values and tradition. Seated in a circle around the family table, the children learned to recite their prayers, to sing the songs their parents had learned in their own childhood, and heard, countless times, nostalgic accounts of life in the old-country village. Home education was conducted informally; booklearning was beyond the capabilities of most parents. But if there was a literate person in the household — one of the parents, or an older child who had attended a village school for a' year or two before coming to Canada — he taught the youngsters to read and write. The teaching aid might be an old Ukrainian school primer that had been packed into the immigrant trunk along with the family's other possessions, a newspaper, or whatever might be on hand.

Few families were spared the tragedy of losing a child. These stones, standing side by side in a Smoky Lake cemetery, mark the graves of three children from a single family. Two died as infants; the third, as a child of four.

Mary Shewchuk It was very rare to find a book in the house in those days. Many people didn't know how to read, and even those who did couldn't afford to buy books. My grandmother taught my mother to read Ukrainian by using an old calendar.

The joy of closely-knit family life brought solace to the immigrants. But there was tragedy too.

Mrs. Kucheran Children used to die so much. One of my sisters died of the mumps. My parents never thought of taking her to a doctor.

The death of small children was a common fact of pioneer life. Today, so many of the deaths would seem needless. Not only serious diseases, like diphtheria and pneumonia, but even routine childhood illnesses — mumps, measles, flu — regularly took their toll in young victims. Illness was commonly the result of poverty combined with ignorance of proper health practices. During the lean early years, poor nutrition was more the norm than the exception among Ukrainian immigrants. Youngsters often lacked clothing sufficient to protect them from the harsh prairie climate. On the coldest of winter days, small children might wander outside clad only in light coats and thin pairs of shoes. To make matters worse, the crowded conditions of the settlers' dwellings made isolation of the sick from the healthy impossible. If one child fell ill, all the others were exposed to danger.

The benefits of medical care, meagre as they were at the turn of the century, were unknown to the settlers. When a child was struck by illness, the parents were far more likely to fall back on their knowledge of folk medicine than to go for a doctor. Not only were doctors scarce and the money to pay them even scarcer, but there was no tradition among the peasants of reliance on professional care. The mother of the sick child nursed him as best she could, with herbs, garlic, berries or tea. If the child died, its death was accepted as God's will. Generations of harsh peasant life had bred into the Ukrainians an attitude of resignation in the face of tragedy. Death — even of an innocent child — was seen as an act of God over which man had no control.

No sooner had the Ukrainians begun to arrive in Canada than tiny graves began to appear in the community cemeteries. Within a few years, some unfortunate families already had three or four small plots, side by side, marked with simple crosses as the resting place of their children.

Community Life

Strong bonds of co-operation existed not only within individual families, but within whole communities. Close ties between neighbours had always been a feature of village life; now they were strengthened even more by necessity. In a country where sheer physical survival was not guaranteed, there was an absolute need for solidarity.

The colonies of Ukrainian settlers that were strung out across the western provinces were largely self-sufficient, not only materially but culturally and socially as well. Isolated from the mainstream of Canadian society by their language, their customs and the hostility of the dominant anglophone population, the Ukrainians reacted in the most natural way — by sticking together. Having been left to struggle alone from the moment they stepped off the immigrant trains, the settlers knew that little help could be expected from the "guberman." Out of fear and ignorance of Canadian ways, the people shied away even from those social and legal agencies that might have given them some assistance.

Pearl Strynadka   People didn't call the police if something happened. They were used from the Old Country to be afraid of the police. One man here had a wife who suddenly disappeared. People thought he killed her because he was selling off her clothes. But nobody said anything to the police. Years later, a man who bought the land dug up a skull. It turned out to be the wife's. Now it was sure the husband killed her, but he was somewhere far away by then.

Internal problems, disagreements, even crimes suspected or committed, were rarely reported to the authorities. Under Austrian rule in their native provinces, the people had learned to regard all figures of authority — police, military, government officials — with fear and suspicion, for they knew only too well that the function of officials was not to help the powerless peasants, but only to oppress them. This deeply rooted attitude of fear and mistrust remained with the immigrants during their first years in Canada.

So the Ukrainian settlers relied upon each other. As much as their frontier existence would allow, they came together for family visits and larger social gatherings. Socializing brought much-needed relief from the grim reality of the homestead, and enabled the settlers to commiserate with each other in their misfortune, forgetting their present circumstances, if only for the moment, while they sang, laughed and reminisced about better days in the past.

Anastasia Zazula People were so poor long ago, but still they could be happy. On holidays someone always visited. They would sit together and talk. The men would play flutes, the women would sing.

And people came together for help in matters big and small.

Bill Shandro My father learned how to read and write when he was a boy. I remember people would always be coming to our house to ask him to read their letters from home, and write letters back. He was always happy to do it.

Rags hung out in a farmyard, lights set out in a farmhouse window — signs that help was needed — were never ignored by passersby. After all, every settler knew the day might come when he too would need assistance. If illness or accidental injury rendered a man incapable of work, his neighbours pitched in to do his seeding or harvesting. If his buildings burned down, his family could always find temporary shelter with other settlers.

Misfortune wasn't confined to individuals. Sometimes whole communities bent under the blow of tragedy. The most dreadful and devastating was the Spanish influenza epidemic that raged through

Canada and around the world in 1918. In the Ukrainian colonies, the death toll from this disease was enormous. How many families were left childless, how many children lost one or both parents, is impossible to estimate. In each district a communal effort was mounted to deal with the epidemic. All those who were well joined forces with doctors, midwives and religious personnel to attend to the sick. Most often, their efforts met with little success.

Mrs. Snihor My father was the only man around here who didn't get the flu. He took care of all his neighbours. He brought them food, delivered their mail, went for the doctor. The doctor visited the sick, but there wasn't much he could do. So many people died. So many children were left without parents.

Sister Servant People were dying so much they were sometimes buried five to a grave. There was only one man in the whole district who had a car then. He would drive around and pick up the sick then bring them to Mundare to our convent. The sisters treated them with home medicines. They gave them alcohol spirits and put heated bricks on their bodies. We were very fortunate. 300 people were saved here, and not one sister died.

In just that one year of 1918, the number of crosses in the rural cemeteries mounted dramatically.

The flu, numerous other diseases and homestead accidents left many children orphaned during the pioneer era. Whenever possible, the children remained in the community, in the homes of relatives or friends. Those who had nowhere to go were often taken in by the Church. In 1913 the Sister Servants built an orphanage in Mundare. The annals of the Ukrainian Catholic mission in Mundare record many instances of helpless orphaned children arriving at the Sisters' doorstep:

***Mundare Yesterday and Today*,**
Mundare: Basilian Fathers,
1969, p. 122.

The priest comes back from his mission travels . . . and brings with him two children, brother and sister. The father has died, the mother is very ill. . . . They found this small boy by a corpse of a dead mother. He was brought by the priest to the sisters. They didn't know if this boy was baptized, so they baptized him conditionally. He was baptized on St. Thomas' Sunday, and therefore was named Thomas.

Not long after their arrival, the Ukrainian immigrants began to organize themselves in their new homeland. In the space of a few years a variety of associations, religious, cultural and political, had

This bookstore served the Ukrainian community of Smoky Lake, Alberta.

sprung up. Most of these were based in the cities, in part because the more literate, socially-conscious immigrants tended to settle in urban centres, but also because it was easier for people to come together in cities than in the countryside, where long distances, lack of roads and the constant demands of work on the homestead stood in the way of organized activity. During the first years of this century, Ukrainians in Winnipeg and Edmonton formed numerous reading associations, amateur dramatic groups and choirs, to provide cultural enrichment for their people, and educational and self-help groups aimed at teaching English to new arrivals and helping them adjust to life in a foreign land.

Even in the rural settlements, some activity was brewing. At first, most organizations were religious in nature, but some cultural groups were launched too. As early as 1897 a reading association was formed at the Edna colony. Similar associations, whose purpose was to organize libraries and bring people together to read or be read to, were set up in Canora, Saskatchewan in 1907, in Ladywood, Manitoba in 1908, and in Myrnam, Alberta in 1909. In some regions — Edna and Vegreville, for example — the work-weary settlers even mustered the energy to put on theatrical performances for their countrymen. In their enthusiasm, they found time between chores on the homestead to attend rehearsals, to memorize their lines — some of the actors, being illiterate, couldn't even read the original text themselves — and to make their own costumes.

A result of this wide-scale movement towards organization was the development of a Ukrainian-language press, including the pioneering *Canadian Farmer*, established in 1903, in Winnipeg. Shortly thereafter, a great number of periodicals burst forth, reflecting almost every conceivable stripe of religious and political opinion. There were Catholic newspapers (*Canadian Ruthenian*, Winnipeg, 1911), Orthodox newspapers (*Orthodox Ruthenian*, Mundare, 1911) and publications issued in Ukrainian by the English Protestant churches (*Morning*, 1905). Some supported the Liberal party (*Canadian Farmer*); others the Conservative (*The Word*, Winnipeg, 1904). Some espoused an independent position (*The News*, Edmonton, 1913); still others were socialist (*The Red Banner*, Winnipeg, 1907). Most originated in cities, with Winnipeg taking the lead as the publication centre. But even in some rural colonies presses were set into motion: in Rosthern, Saskatchewan (*The New Country*, 1910); in Wostok, Alberta (*Warning*, 1912); and in Mundare, Alberta (*Progress*, 1915).

This diversified native language press gave the immigrants a greatly needed source of information about events in their new country, and a vehicle for expressing their views and opinions on those matters which most concerned them. The newspapers and periodicals also carried the earliest literature produced by Ukrainians in Canada: poems and stories describing the immigrant experience.

A small number of Ukrainians already possessed a high degree of political awareness when they arrived in Canada.

Mike Novakowsky My father was interested in politics. He was a radical. He even spoke at political meetings during the first election after he came here. And that was before he had the right to vote.

But among the mass of the people political consciousness was limited. Unused to exercising power, absorbed by their work on the homestead, they paid little attention to the political processes of their new country. Although they acquired the right to vote upon becoming Canadian citizens, they did not strive to use this power to their advantage. And as "foreigners" they were largely ignored by the politicians — except, of course, at election time. Then interest in these new citizens would suddenly mount, as pioneer teacher, W.A. Czumer recounts in his memoirs:

Czumer, p. 116, *Whenever federal, provincial or local elections rolled around, all sorts*
(author's translation). *of political agents travelled through the colonies instructing the new citizens how to vote and who to vote for.*

It often happened that in the morning a farmer would receive a visit from one political agent, who would urge him to vote for Harrison, because Harrison is a fine man. That same evening, another agent would arrive and tell the farmer that Harrison is a "so and so," and that all "Ruthenians" should vote for Ferguson, because it was Ferguson's party that brought them to Canada.

These "lessons" in Canadian democratic procedure were often lubricated by generous amounts of whisky provided at the expense of the hopeful candidate.

To the more enlightened Ukrainians it was clear that their people would carry little political clout until they participated more directly in the democratic process. The first Ukrainian to put himself forth as a candidate in an election was Vasyl Holowacky, who ran for Parliament as a socialist in the Selkirk, Manitoba riding in 1911. He received a bare 146 votes. It was in Alberta, in 1913, that the first concerted political effort on the part of Ukrainians took place. The provincial legislature was dissolved that spring and an election called for April 17. The leaders of the Alberta Ukrainian community decided the time was ripe to try fielding Ukrainian candidates. Several ridings east of Edmonton had large Ukrainian populations. By sheer strength of numbers Ukrainians were in a position to elect three or four of their own representatives. But only one Ukrainian, Andrew Shandro, succeeded in winning an official party nomination. Shandro was chosen to run as the Liberal candidate in Whitford, the constituency that had the highest concentration of Ukrainian voters in the province.

Disappointed by the lack of support for Ukrainians on the part of the established parties, four other prominent Ukrainians had declared themselves independent candidates in ridings heavily populated by Ukrainian immigrants. When the election took place, only Andrew Shandro was victorious. He sat in the Alberta Legislature from 1913 to 1921, the first Ukrainian in Canada to hold an elected office beyond the local level. His election was a step on the long road that was eventually to lead to full participation by the Ukrainians in the political life of this country.

Milestones

Birth When it came to bearing children, the immigrant woman couldn't afford to be fainthearted or helpless. There was no question of giving birth in the comfortable sterile surroundings of a hospital. The woman had her children at home, on the homestead, sometimes alone, for her husband might well be away at work. If she had access to any help at all, it was that of a midwife, not a doctor.

Three generations of Ukrainian settlers in Canada.

In an age when medical facilities were almost non-existent, an experienced midwife was a valued member of the rural community. Among the Ukrainian settlers were a number of women who had practiced midwifery in their native villages. In Canada their skills proved most useful.

Eva Kretzul My mother learned to be a midwife in the Old Country. I was too young to notice everything she did, but I remember that she used to make all her own medicines at home. She used a lot of goosefat, and she kept a special supply of moonshine that was distilled twice. Then, if she had to make a cut during the delivery, she would rub that moonshine on the spot where she cut, to make it numb.

Every time she delivered a baby my mother made a knot in a ball of yarn. She always carried that yarn with her. When she died, she had two balls like that, full of knots. In all those years she was a midwife, she didn't lose one mother or baby.

A good midwife inevitably found her services much in demand. Rarely would a week go by without some distraught husband coming to fetch her to attend to his wife, most likely at a homestead miles away from her own. When a call came, the midwife dropped whatever she was doing, packed her obstetrical aids, and went off to the house of the labouring woman. There she stayed, not only during the birth but for at least one day following, to ascertain that all was going well, and to relieve the new mother of her household chores. For her trouble, the midwife was paid according to the family's means.

Unfortunately, a midwife who lost not a single mother or child was the rare exception, not the rule. In the western Canada of the early 1900s, childbirth was hazardous. The mortality rate among mothers at that time was more than thirty times what it is today. However skilled and conscientious the midwife might be, there were factors beyond her control that could easily result in the deaths of mothers, infants, or both: unsterile conditions in pioneer houses was a factor, as was the weakened state of mothers who were overworked, undernourished and often already worn down by numerous earlier childbirths.

As a rule, even the poorest settlers regarded the birth of a new child if not with joy, then at least with calm acceptance. Every infant was a blessing from God, another family member who would some day help with the farmwork and look after his parents in their old age. Soon after the birth, arrangements were made for baptism. A pair of reliable relatives or friends were selected to stand as godparents, and, as soon as the services of a priest could be secured, the infant was taken to church. Once the religious ceremony was over, the happy event was celebrated at home, with a baptismal dinner attended by the godparents, the priest and close friends of the family.

Marriage For the young girl growing up on the homestead, there was no opportunity for advanced education, no prospects for independent work. By the time she reached the age of fifteen, sixteen, seventeen, she was deemed ready for marriage. Her formal schooling — if she

A winter wedding in Alberta.

had any at all – was over. She had spent several years helping her parents with their farmwork and learning from her mother the essential household skills of cooking, sewing, spinning, weaving and embroidery. Now, under the strict guidance of her parents, it was time to make arrangements for marriage.

During the first phase of the Ukrainians' life in Canada, the social customs of the village still held sway. In matters of marriage, parental authority reigned. A daughter was instructed when to marry, and, not uncommonly, whom to marry. At an age when she had barely outgrown her interest in childish games the girl might be less than eager to go to the altar, but unless she was prepared to take the drastic step of running away from home – and a few did – she complied with her parents' wishes.

A suitable match was made and the date for the wedding set. Tradition limited the times when weddings could take place: they were forbidden during all the lengthy periods of fast. Only after thirty or forty years in this country did the settlers begin to disregard these restrictions and hold marriages in all seasons, a move that deeply shocked and scandalized the older generation.

All residents of the district were expected to join in the wedding festivities. Invitations were extended not by mail, but in person. The families of the young couple went from homestead to homestead, inviting their neighbours to attend the celebration. Invariably, the invitation was accepted. No matter how pressing the responsibilities of running a farm might be, nobody was ever too busy to come to a wedding.

The traditional Ukrainian wedding was a long and elaborate ceremony, combining ancient folk customs and religious rites. Among immigrants on foreign soil, the rituals were of necessity somewhat simplified and abbreviated, but still the wedding, including preparations and separate celebrations at the homes of both parties, took up the best part of a week. The schedule of events went something like this:

Monday: The bride and her attendants prepare the special wedding loaves and make a ceremonial headdress out of flowers and herbs for the bride to wear on her wedding day. For the groom, they make a smaller wreath, to be worn on his hat or his lapel.

Wednesday: A gay and lively dance is held for the young friends of the bride and groom. This is the young couple's last outing as carefree, unmarried people.

Thursday: Dressed in their finest clothes and ceremonial wreaths, the bride and groom go to church to be married. Before they set out, they are blessed by their parents. Following the religious ceremony, the bride and the groom return separately to the homes of their respective parents. In each house a party is held for guests invited by the family. In the evening the groom, accompanied by a party of attendants and relatives, comes to fetch the bride. He takes her back to his parents' house, where celebrations are going at full tilt.

Friday: A day of family celebrations. The parents of the bride come to the home of the groom. The bride is ceremoniously dressed as a married woman.

Sunday: The groom's family visits the parents of the bride.

Scores of wagons congregated at the homesteads of the bride and the groom, carrying guests from all around. Everyone was dressed for the occasion in his best garb. Instead of gifts, the women each brought a live chicken, the men, a loaf of bread. These food offerings helped compensate the hosts for the food they used in preparing the wedding feast. If any chickens were left over, the young couple took them to start a flock of their own.

Mrs. Kowalchuk   When the wedding guests came from miles away, they would spend the night. How they found room for so many people in those little houses, I don't know. They would put blankets on the dirt floor, lie down in rows and sleep. When my older sister got married, all the ladies stayed up all night killing chickens, plucking them and cooking them. They talked and sang as they worked.

The tiny pioneer houses rocked and creaked as they filled up with crowds of people. In one corner sat the musicians, playing rousing dance music on violins, dulcimers and flutes. The guests ate, drank, sang and danced the night away, happy to break away for a time from the daily routine of farm chores. Fortunately, the hosts could always rely on neighbours to help in the preparation of food and in the unpleasant job of cleaning up after the departure of the guests.

After marriage, many young couples lived for a time in the parental home, usually that of the groom. Once they were in a position to establish themselves on a homestead, or buy an existing farm, they moved away to start a separate family life of their own.

Death Rural people were on familiar terms with death. They saw it come often, for the young and for the old. Like birth, death took place at home, in the presence of the whole family.

When a settler died, his body lay at home for a period of three days. During this time, he was washed and attired in his best clothes. Members of his own family, or a local carpenter, made a coffin, a plain wooden box. In the little church cemetery a grave was dug. If the death occurred in winter, a fire was built first on the grave site, to thaw out the ground.

On the third day, the deceased was laid to rest. All the settlers in the district turned out at the church, somberly dressed, in order to mourn the departed man, woman or child, and to comfort the family who suffered the loss. After the funeral, all were invited to the home of the bereaved family to partake of a memorial dinner. As he left for home, each guest was given a loaf to take back with him in memory of the dead person.

The Ukrainian settlers respected and remembered their dead. Each family erected simple white homemade crosses on the graves of their loved ones. They took pains to keep the graves neat and free of weeds, and the crosses freshly painted. The anniversary of each death was commemorated. Forty days after the funeral, a second memorial meal was given; on the first anniversary, a third. Even the seventh anniversary of the death was remembered in this way.

After Easter, the whole community remembered its dead collectively, with a religious ritual known as *provody*. All the settlers gathered in the churchyard with baskets of food which they placed on their family graves. The priest walked through the cemetery, blessing the graves and the food, while the congregation walked in procession behind him. Then each family sat down beside the graves of their own dead to eat, in their "presence," the blessed meal.

The funeral of an elderly pioneer woman at Smoky Lake.

School Days

Not the least of the attractions that Canada held out to the hapless European immigrants was free access for all to education. But this right wasn't one the newcomers would begin to enjoy very quickly. No little red schoolhouse sat waiting for them in the western woodlands. A good many years would pass before most Ukrainian children would first set foot inside a Canadian schoolroom.

The sole exceptions were children of immigrants homesteading in regions already well-populated by earlier settlers. In the area of the Edna/Star colony, for example, the more established English and German settlers were able to build schools by the mid-1890s. Ukrainian children attended these schools too, and, according to immigration official Speers, their progress was good:

C. W. Speers;
Kaye, p. 347.

There are two schools already established on the colony, one at Limestone Lake, and the other at Beaver Creek, which are open eight months in the year. These colonists are very anxious to learn our language, and are keeping their children at school, where they have

A one-room school in Alberta. This one was built in 1911 in the Quiet Nook school district.

had an opportunity and in all cases the teachers speak highly of the progress of the pupils — they are quick, bright and attentive.

But in the colonies that were almost exclusively Ukrainian — and these were in the majority — education developed at a much slower pace. Initially, the settlers were far too absorbed by the need for survival to think seriously about their children's schooling. They didn't even know how to go about organizing schools, and they would have been hard pressed to find the funds needed to do so. In the meantime, children were growing up without the benefits of education.

Mr. Basaraba I was eight years old when we came to Canada. That was 1902. There was no school in the district until 1912. So I never went. At sixteen I had to go out and work on the railroad.

A whole generation of children missed formal schooling almost entirely. In the worst position were the ones who emigrated as youngsters of ten years or less. They were too young to have gone to school in their native villages, too old to go in Canada. By the time schools began to appear in their settlements, these children were in their teens. They were the ones parents singled out to stay behind on the farm or to go out to work, while their luckier younger brothers

An English school teacher who had taught in some of the poorest "foreign districts" wrote about her students: "Galician children came to school in filthy, tattered, patch-upon-patch clothes. Nails were used instead of buttons. Shoes were laced up with binder twine. They appear miserable with an aged complexion, overworked and tired faces, without the least desire to participate in children's games." (*Mundare Yesterday and Today*, p. 104).

and sisters were sent off to school to probe the mysteries of reading, writing and arithmetic.

A small effort to fill the educational void in the new colonies was launched by the Ukrainian Catholic Church, and by various English Protestant churches who took it upon themselves to set up missions in the poor "Galician" settlements. They operated private schools, in which a limited number of children boarded and received instruction. One such school, situated a few miles north of Smoky Lake, was Kolokreeka (literally, "by the creek"), so named because of its location on the banks of the White Earth Creek. Another was a school established in 1903 by the Sister Servants of Mundare. The Sisters' school attracted children from Ukrainian colonies near and far. They lived, learned and worked together in the convent, crammed in several to a bed, and even bedded down on the floor.

Sister Servant   Most people were very eager for their children to go to school. Children would come from all over to our school. Some even came from Saskatchewan. Once, two children — a little brother and sister — arrived at the school. They walked barefoot all the way from Innisfree. They carried their shoes so that they wouldn't wear them out. Many families could not afford to pay for the school. Some children would catch muskrats to pay for their school supplies. Many would do jobs around the convent to earn their keep.

For some time the private schools offered at least a small number of Ukrainian children a chance at education. But as the number of local schools grew, the need for private schools subsided. At its peak, the sisters' school housed 111 children. By 1918, with a government program underway to build public schools every six miles, the enrolment had shrunk to 62.

The years were slipping by, and the more forward looking Ukrainian settlers were concerned to see their children growing up in ignorance. To them, the benefits of education, and of learning the language of their new country, were apparent. Clearly, the time had come to build schools. Inevitably, a minority of residents in any given area resisted the idea. They had a lot of land now — why waste money on schools? As long as their sons learned how to plough, they reasoned, and their daughters how to sew and cook, nothing more was needed. But the matter could be postponed no longer. With the help of government-appointed school organizers, meetings were called, plans were laid, school trustees were elected. This is how education came to the children in one colony, the Shandro district of Alberta:

Bill Shandro   People began coming into this area in 1899. By 1905 the district was quite settled. But there was still no school for us children, so my father called a meeting at our house about building a school. All the farmers came. There were some that didn't want a school because they would have to pay taxes. "We came here to get away from all those taxes," they said. But when they heard that their children had to go to school or they might have to pay a fine, they changed their minds fast. Then everyone wanted a school.

The school opened in April, 1907. Our first teacher came from near Camrose. He came to our house first because my father was chairman of the school board.

When school started I was 10 years old. I remember the first few days very well. The teacher opened a big trunk and pulled out some pictures. First there was a picture of a horse. So all the kids said "kin," in Ukrainian. The teacher said "horse." We repeated "horse." Then he took out other pictures: cat, dog, boy, girl. We repeated the words after him. In about two weeks we could speak some English.

Year by year, more and more new school districts bearing characteristically Ukrainian names began to spread out across the prairies. In each district, the first responsibility of the rate payers was to erect a school building; the second, to hire a teacher. A standard plan for a one-room schoolhouse was supplied by the Departments of Education. For reasons of economy, the residents of most communities hauled logs and put up the buildings themselves. But the second step wasn't so easy: to find a teacher willing to come to the new school. Well-qualified teachers didn't rush to sign on to the unpopular "foreign districts." Given a choice, why should they take on the arduous job of teaching children who knew not a word of English, in a remote area where the salary was low and the teacher's living conditions — room and board in the overcrowded house of a local family — far from desirable? With a few exceptions, the Ukrainian school boards had to content themselves with hiring uncertified teachers, many of them young boys, still students themselves, who had been granted temporary teaching permits.

The rural school began its life on a part-time basis. Ratepayers couldn't afford to pay the teacher's salary — $50 to $70 per month in the pre-war years — for many months at a time. Lack of money, added to difficulties of transportation, resulted in shortened school terms that lasted only four to six months of the year. Schools opened their doors in April or May, closed them again in the fall as the cold weather approached. There were no roads from the homesteads to the schools. For most children, the only means of transportation was their feet. It was hard enough in summer for them to tramp their way to school through mud and bush; in winter it was impossible.

The children who turned out at a new school on opening day were a ragtag bunch. They came from all directions, on foot, on horseback, by ox-driven cart. The pupils registering in grade one ranged from tiny tots of seven to strapping youths of fourteen who towered well over the head of their teacher. To the teacher they must have appeared a strange and sorry sight: a motley array of children dressed in the best clothes their parents could find for the occasion — mainly hand-me-downs, some too large, others too small, nearly all patched and patched again. A few children came outfitted in shoes or boots belonging to parents or older siblings, for they had none of their own. Even more were barefoot. All sat and gaped at the stranger, the new teacher, with a mixture of curiosity and apprehension.

How was the teacher to instruct a room full of children who spoke only Ukrainian? Some, like the teacher at Shandro, relied on pictures to begin communication. The ubiquitous Eaton's catalogue, with its handy combination of words and illustrations, saw use in many schools across the prairies as a first reader. Through incentive or punishment, the teachers strove to induce their pupils to speak English.

Mrs. Kowalchuk We didn't know any English when we started school. Our teacher didn't allow us to speak Ukrainian during recess. Some of the children would spy. If someone spoke Ukrainian they would run and tell the teacher. Then he would make us sit in the corner. This was very hard on us at first, but then we got better at English and it wasn't so bad.

Student attendance was spotty. When work on the homestead was slow, they came regularly. But at the peak seasons of the farm calendar — seeding and harvest time — hardly a child would show his face in the schoolroom. In addition, girls, whose education was held in less regard than the boys', were often kept at home to assist their overworked mothers. School had to take a second place to the farm.

Mrs. Kowalchuk   I was twelve or thirteen when I started school at Desjarlais. I stayed for two years. Then I had to leave. My parents needed me. So I never went past grade two.

The country school didn't go beyond grade eight. Any bright student who wanted to go further was obliged to transfer to a town high school. But in the first years, very few did. The average family couldn't afford to spare a good worker, or to pay the upkeep of a student living away from home. In fact, even those who reached the eighth grade were rare. With so many students starting school at an advanced age, the drop-out rate in the earliest grades was high. According to a 1915 report on the bilingual districts of Manitoba, 68 per cent of the Ukrainian and Polish school population was enrolled in grades one and two, while only 2 per cent could be found above grade five. (C. K. Newcombe, *Report to the Minister of Education;* Manoly Lupul, "The Ukrainians and Public Education," not yet published, p. 12).

The Battle for Bilingual Schools

With regard to education in the so-called "foreign belt" of western Canada, immigration official Speers wrote:

Kaye, p. 174.   *The establishment of schools among these people is a very important matter, which I trust will receive attention in the proper quarter. The people are very anxious to learn our language and ways and this is particularly the case with Galicians who have even adopted Canadian dress and discarded their traditional costumes. They will soon become absorbed in our Canadian nationality. . . .*

The view of Mr. Speers, many provincial educational authorities, and most of the Anglo-Canadian public at large, was that schools in two Ukrainian school girls. Would these children be taught in English only, or would Ukrainian also be admitted as a language of instruction? This question was at the centre of the struggle waged by the immigrant community against the government establishment in all three prairie provinces. With regard to the situation in Saskatchewan, where for some years other language instruction was permitted for one hour per day, the *Canadian Ruthenian* wrote: "The English chauvinists cannot sleep from "worry" that in "foreign" schools it is still possible to teach for an hour, not in English, but in a language spoken by a mother to her child. They "fear" that "single hour" more than a Hunnish invasion." (Winnipeg, Feb. 1918; Lupul, "The Ukrainians and Public Education," p. 30).

immigrant colonies should serve as vehicles for speedy assimilation. In a report compiled in Saskatchewan in 1916, Dr. Anderson, school inspector for the Yorkton area, urged that immigrant children be taught by "good strong types of Canadian manhood and womanhood" who would mould their young charges to fit "Canadian life and ideals."(*Annual Report of the Department of Education of the Province of Saskatchewan* 1916, p. 142; Lupul, p. 24).

But the Ukrainians themselves had other ideas. By and large, they favoured a system of bilingual education, in which their children would be instructed by Ukrainian-speaking teachers. In such a system, they believed, their children would not only learn their native tongue, they would even master English more quickly, for the communication barriers between pupils and teachers would be eliminated.

In fact, regulations in all three prairie provinces allowed a certain amount of other-language instruction. The laws in Manitoba were most generous; in this province, full-scale bilingual education was permitted in any language in conjunction with English. Nevertheless, the struggle of the Ukrainian settlers to maintain bilingual education in their schools was doomed to failure. There were two insurmountable obstacles. The first was an acute shortage of qualified bilingual teachers in all three provinces, which the establishment of special training schools (the Ruthenian Training School, Winnipeg, 1905, the Training School for Teachers for Foreign Speaking Communities, Regina, 1909, and the Training School for Foreigners, Vegreville, 1913) did little to alleviate.

The second barrier was the bitter and ever-mounting opposition to the principle of bilingualism on the part of some government members, Protestant church groups and the anglophone press. This hostility reached its height during the First World War, when, in the name of Canadian patriotism, backlash against foreigners grew to border on hysteria. By the time the war came to a close, the Ukrainian language had been banned from classrooms all across the prairies.

The question of bilingualism aroused considerable furore in all three provinces, but nowhere more than in Alberta, where it became closely linked with provincial party politics. The conflict came in the aftermath of the controversial provincial election of 1913, in which the Ukrainians had fielded four candidates of their own. The Liberal party establishment, which had traditionally enjoyed the support of Ukrainian voters, was displeased by this show of independence. The blame for the agitation was put on the shoulders of the province's bilingual teachers. Such was the view promulgated by the Liberal party press, including the *Vegreville Observer*, which wrote, in the exaggerated, inflammatory style that characterized western journalism of the day:

Vegreville Observer, September 10, 1913; Czumer, p. 135.

In all these disturbances the Ruthenian teachers were taking the lead. After the election, many of them remained in Alberta in order to prolong their Conservative and separatist activities. These Ruthenian teachers have only one idea, and that is to instruct the children and parents that as they were persecuted in Galicia by Polacks, in Russia by Russians, so they are persecuted in Canada by English fanatics; at election time their idea is to work against the Government. We all saw teachers Czumer, Sytnik, Bozik, Mykytiuk, etc. on the platforms at Vegreville and Mundare talking to the people and telling them that "the rule of English cowboys is finished; we are now in charge; we are a nation able to govern our own matters," etc.

Within a month after the election, the Minister of Education, John Boyle, punished the teachers for their "Conservative and separatist activities" by revoking, overnight, their temporary teaching permits. Thirteen teachers suddenly found themselves fired from their jobs. Boyle's arbitrary move angered the Ukrainian community, and led to a bitter anti-Boyle campaign that was spearheaded by the Edmonton-based Ukrainian newspaper, the *News*. When government-appointed school trustee Robert Fletcher began to bring English teachers into formerly bilingual schools, the ratepayers of two school districts, Kolomea and Stanislawiw, refused to accept them. For their trouble, they were taken to court and ordered to pay a fine. The members of a third Ukrainian school district, Bukovina, went even further. They simply ignored the Boyle-approved teacher who came to their school, built a private school of their own nearby, and continued to retain the services of their bilingual teacher, W. Czumer.

Boyle and his supporters were outraged. The Liberal party mouthpiece, the *Edmonton Bulletin*, jumped into the fray, lashing out against the Ukrainians and supporting Boyle's position of English supremacy. An article printed on August 20, 1913, stated:

Edmonton Bulletin;
Czumer, pp. 126-27.

A number of Galicians who had been employed in Manitoba schools came here last spring and were at once installed by the Galician school boards.

It is stated that many of these so-called teachers were scarcely able to speak and write English. . . . In Manitoba the Galicians were allowed to get control of their schools with the result that children are growing up in the province unable to speak a word of English. Mr. Boyle emphatically declared that no such state of affairs would be permitted in Alberta.

"This is an English-speaking province" said Mr. Boyle, "and every Alberta boy and girl should receive a sound English education in the public schools of this province."

The editor of the *News*, Roman Kremar, never one to back away from a fight, countered two days later with a slamming indictment of Boyle and the forces of "anglicization." Under the dramatic headline "The Liberals Declare War on the Ukrainians," he wrote:

The News,
August 22, 1913;
Czumer, pp. 129-133,
(author's translation).

The honourable Minister of Education lies when he appeals to the pride of English jingoists, telling them that in Alberta schools languages other than English are forbidden. Paragraph 139 of the School Ordinance says that teaching is permitted in any language that the parents might desire.

The honourable Minister of Education lies when he says that Alberta is an English province. Alberta is a Canadian province, in which all nationalities have equal rights, including the Ukrainians, who are one of the most numerous groups.

Furthermore, the Minister of Education lies shamelessly when he says the teachers from Manitoba can't speak English. . . . How dare Mr. Boyle contend that an experienced teacher and a university student aren't capable of speaking English?

The Ukrainians haven't opposed and don't oppose the English language. Ukrainians want to know English, and the more they know it the better. Ukrainians would be the first to get rid of any teacher who came to teach at their schools not knowing English. . . .

We're ready to supply witnesses who heard from Mr. Boyle's own lips that "We're keeping the schools in Alberta for our friends." Anyone who understands the machinations of Alberta Liberals doesn't need to be told who these "friends" are and why the Manitoba teachers don't fit into that category. Now the cat's out of the bag! It's not so much the English language that the Minister of Education is so concerned about, as the interests of the Liberal party.

But Kremar's passionate rhetoric and pressure by Ukrainian groups notwithstanding, the battle was already lost. The school trustees of Bukovina were taken to court and fined for continuing to pay their Ukrainian teacher. At the close of 1913 Boyle brought in an amendment to the School Act which rendered the private school at Bukovina illegal. Only one more incident took place before the matter was finally closed. When Mr. Armstrong, the English teacher who had twiddled his thumbs at Bukovina for several months, returned from his Christmas holiday in January, 1914, he received a visit from a delegation of local women who asked him to leave their district. A scuffle ensued, as a result of which one woman was charged with assault and sentenced to a prison term of two months. On that unhappy note, the affair was ended.

Bilingual education for Ukrainian immigrant children was quashed in Alberta in 1913. It ceased to exist in Manitoba in 1916 and in Saskatchewan in 1918. In none of these provinces would the issue surface again for several decades.

Children at Toporoutz school in Alberta. This school district was established in 1909.

Learning in a One-room School

John Strynadka It was a one-room school. Some of the children had to walk five miles to get there. We had 83 children going at the time, all in one room. It was very hard for the teachers. Two years was the most any teacher would stay.

A one-room wooden building constructed to a standard plan, surrounded by a yard of two or three acres; next to it, a tiny teacherage: this was the rural school.

Inside the classroom stood several rows of small double desks for students, a larger desk for the teacher and a blackboard. Once the school began to operate on a year-round basis, a pot-bellied, wood-burning stove took its place in one corner of the room.

There were no sophisticated teaching aids to help stave off boredom and speed the process of learning. At the beginning of term, each pupil was issued a slate, a slate pencil and two or three textbooks — for many children, the first books they had ever possessed.

There was no gymnasium, no sports equipment, no art supplies. Recreation took the form of improvised games and, in warm weather, softball competitions. On cold and rainy days, teacher and students stayed inside during recess and lunch breaks, singing songs. The highlight of the year was the Christmas concert.

The teacher who took a job in an immigrant school district was faced with more than just the usual problems of trying to inculcate the principles of reading, spelling and mathematics into the heads of young children. A variety of social, economic and cultural hurdles stood in the way of learning. Ukrainian children started school with no knowledge of English. There were children who were undernourished, children who were inadequately clothed, children who were too tired from their daily farm chores to concentrate on their lessons. Eight grades were crammed into one room, students whose size, age and rate of progress varied considerably. Absenteeism was a chronic problem.

Under these conditions it was hard to teach and hard to learn. It's a wonder any progress was made at all. In fact, the quality of education varied from one school to the next, depending above all on the good will and dedication of the teacher. Teachers who regarded posts in immigrant districts as a way of passing time, who stayed a month or two, then moved on to greener pastures, left their charges no wiser than they found them. But under the care of teachers who were patient and devoted to their work, children often made dramatic strides. Their English improved from day to day. Bright students who started school at an older age went through two or three grades in one year. Occasionally, an exceptional student not only completed the eighth grade, but went to high school.

Eva Kretzul I was lucky that the school was one mile away. Some of the children had to walk as far as six miles. It was hard to learn in those old schools. We didn't know English, and there were eight or nine grades with only one teacher. I spent two and a half years in grade one. It took me two years to learn how to read.

Victoria Zaharia The school was two miles from us. In the winter we drove our children to school with oxen. The children didn't have very good clothes. I had to put several different layers of clothes on them to keep them warm.

Mrs. Homeniuk We didn't have any money to buy paper for our children when they were in school. They did their homework on wrapping paper that we got from the store.

Mary Shewchuk The Ukrainian parents didn't know how to dress their kids properly. In the winter, the Canadian girls used to wear bloomers and long stockings, but my mother had only a sheepskin coat and knee-high lumber socks. She was naked from the knees up, except for a thin skirt. My mother's first teacher was a man, so he didn't try to tell them what to wear. But her grade two teacher was a young woman. When she saw how poorly those Ukrainian girls were dressed, she took them all into the room together and lifted up her skirts to show them what she was wearing underneath. Then she got all the mothers together and told them how to dress their daughters. From then on the girls started wearing underwear and they didn't freeze so much.

Eva Kretzul   We always had enough to eat, but there were no luxuries like fresh fruit. For lunch we took bread sprinkled with sugar, or with bacon, potatoes, or pyrohy from the night before. We carried our lunches in old sugar sacks.

Mary Shewchuk   The school kids used to leave their lunches out on the porch while they were in school. Quite often, by the time they came out for lunch, they would find that gophers or chipmunks had eaten most of their food. Finally, the teacher got them to bring their lunches in tin cans.

A Place to Pray

Mrs. Snihor   When people first came into Saskatchewan, there were no churches. The first thing they did was put up a cross. People would meet every Sunday there to pray.

The Ukrainian peasants were people steeped in religious beliefs and traditions. Like their ancestors for centuries before them, they clung faithfully to their churches — Ukrainian Catholic in Galicia, Orthodox in Bukovina. Condemned to an earthly lot of unremitting hardship and poverty, the villagers turned their eyes heavenward, finding in scrupulous religious practice a source of hope and comfort.

As they prepared to leave their villages for Canadian homesteads, few emigrants stopped to consider the state of the church on the other side of the ocean. There were plenty of more mundane and immediate matters to occupy their minds: property to be sold, trunks to be packed, steamship tickets to be bought. But once they were esconced in their new country, the question of religion began to loom larger. For a full five years from the time the first Ukrainian immigrant families stepped onto Canadian soil, not a single Ukrainian priest came into their midst. The absence of familiar clergy and churches weighed heavily on the spirits of the settlers. Secular existence didn't sit well with people who had grown up under the authority of priests and in the stability provided by an organized religious life. Suddenly

The tiny Catholic church of St. Peter and Paul near Sheho, Saskatchewan was built in 1910. The whole congregation participated in its construction, cutting logs, hauling them to the church site, digging clay for plaster. The people of Sheho were poor. They had no cash to pay the expenses incurred in building their church. So they ploughed the surrounding field, sowed it with wheat and sold their crop in the fall. All profits from the sale went to pay for the church. The parishioners of St. Peter and Paul's continued to grow their communal crop for several summers, until the church debt was cleared.

they found themselves living in a religous vacuum. There was nobody to bless their *paska* (Easter bread), baptize their new-born children and marry their young in the accustomed manner. Their only recourse was to gather in each others' homes on Sundays to pray and sing together.

As Catholics, the immigrants from Galicia came under the hierarchy of the Roman Catholic Church, whose chief representatives in western Canada were Bishop Legal in Alberta and Bishop Langevin in Manitoba. Unfortunately, the Roman Catholics had little knowledge of the Eastern members of their Church. They assumed − wrongly − that these unfamiliar Slavic immigrants would be content with the care of priests of the Latin rite, in particular priests from Polish churches, a few of which already existed in the west. But the bishops failed to take account of the Ukrainians' attachment to their own rite, which, although aligned to Rome, was closer in its external observations to the Eastern Orthodox Church, their historical enmity towards Poles and their traditional suspicion of the Roman brand of Catholicism. The settlers longed for priests who would speak to them in their own language and practice the rite they had always followed.

In addition to this basic misunderstanding between the Roman Catholic establishment and the Ukrainian immigrants, their relations were complicated further by the Church's demand that all Catholic church buildings in Canada be registered in the name of the local

Sachava—one of the oldest Ukrainian Orthodox churches in Alberta.

Roman Catholic bishop. Many Ukrainians looked askance at this regulation, fearing that it would give the dominant Roman Catholic Church too much power over their affairs.

In 1897 the bleak religious picture brightened slightly. In the fall of that year, Father Nestor Dmytriw, a Ukrainian Catholic priest from the United States, came through the colonies of Stuartburn, Manitoba and Edna/Star, Alberta. During the next five years the settlers continued to receive sporadic visits from travelling priests. To the spiritually starved populace, every such visit became a momentous occasion. As soon as the word spread that a service would be held at one of the colonies, people flocked to the site in droves.

The visiting priests said Mass in settlers' houses or under the open sky. They performed multiple baptisms of all the infants that had been born in the area since the previous visit by a priest. They consecrated the cemeteries that were gradually growing up in each community, organized parishes and even encouraged the settlers to set about building churches. But their visits were too few and too far between. By 1900 there were six Ukrainian Catholic churches in western Canada — in Winnipeg, Gonor, Stuartburn and Sifton, Manitoba, and Star and Rabbit Hill in Alberta — but still there was not a single permanently-residing priest.

Into the breach left by an inadequate Ukrainian Church organization, stepped a variety of foreign missionaries. Protestant churches, most notably the Methodist and the Presbyterian, endeavoured to set up missions in the Ukrainian colonies. But the most successful by far were the missionaries propagating the Russian Orthodox faith. These priests, whose efforts were encouraged and supported financially by the Orthodox tsarist regime in Moscow, were already established on the west coast of the United States, in California and Alaska. It took no time at all for them to make their way to the Ukrainian colonies in western Canada.

A pair of these Russian missionaries appeared for the first time at Star in July, 1897. They conducted a service in the farmyard of one of the colonists, Theodore Nemirsky, whose homestead lay near the present-day town of Wostok. Although all the Star colonists had come from Galicia, and were therefore Catholic, Nemirsky and a number of others were impressed by the promises of the Russian priests. If the Ukrainian Catholics were to accept Russian Orthodoxy, that church would supply them, at no cost, with priests who practiced a rite very similar to their own, and who spoke, if not fluent Ukrainian, then at least a broken version of that language. Furthermore — and this was an important point — the Russian Orthodox hierarchy would allow church property to remain in the name of the congregation.

This initial visit by the Russian missionaries turned out to be a historic occasion. The seeds were sown for a religious-political conflict that would literally tear apart the fledgling Ukrainian-Canadian community, pitting neighbour against neighbour, friend against friend and brother against brother. The centre of the storm would be the Edna/Star colony, but its effects would ripple out to other colonies in Alberta and throughout the prairie provinces.

The impact of the Russians' summer visit subsided temporarily in the fall when Father Dmytriw arrived at Star and founded there the first Ukrainian Catholic parish in Canada. Encouraged by his visit and that of another Catholic priest the following year, the settlers joined together enthusiastically to build a church. All winter they cut and hauled logs; by the summer of 1898 the church was completed. But again months went by and no priest appeared. The people were disillusioned. Recalling the liberal offer of the Russian missionaries, some members of the community resolved to act upon it and to adopt the Russian Orthodox religion. They wrote to the mission centre in San Francisco requesting that a priest be sent to live at the colony on a permanent basis.

The Star colony was now split into two factions. In the one camp stood the converts, who criticized the Ukrainian Catholic Church's negligence of its own people and its too-cosy relationship with the Roman Catholic establishment. In the other were the faithful Catholics who deplored their neighbours' rejection of their traditional church and their alignment with Russia, the hated oppressor of the Ukrainian people. The battle lines were drawn; the battle was yet to come.

It broke out on Easter Sunday 1901. Shortly before this day, a Ukrainian Catholic priest came to Alberta; so did a Russian. Each of the two factions invited its own priest to conduct an Easter service in the colony's single church. The clash that resulted is recounted by Father Bozyk in his *History of the Ukrainian Church in Canada*:

Bozyk, p. 20, *The Russian priest, Yakiw Korchinsky, held a service in the church*
(author's translation). *while the Catholic priest, Ivan Zaklynsky, said Mass in the churchyard. During the blessing of the paska and the procession around the church, each side obstructed and goaded the other with shouts. The noise drowned out the religious singing. Women and children were crying. The police kept order and prevented people from fighting.*

From that time on the hatred between people over the question of the church was so deeply rooted that they refused to greet each other when they met. When Ukrainians from other areas passed through on their way to Edmonton, people wouldn't take them in for the night, or even allow them to water their horses if they were members of the rival church. The differences that arose over the church spread out to other colonies. . . .

The disagreement over the ownership of the church at Star didn't remain for long at the level of catcalls and insults. In 1904 the two congregations took their dispute to the courts. The Catholics maintained that at the time of the church's construction, the whole community was still Catholic. If it was built as a Catholic church, they reasoned, it should remain Catholic. The Orthodox splinter group countered that the first service held in the church was an Orthodox one; therefore the church was now Orthodox. The case was first heard in an Edmonton courtroom. From there a series of appeals carried it to the Supreme Court of Canada, and finally, to the Privy Council in London. In June, 1907, the British body ruled that the church belonged to the congregation, that is, the Orthodox faction. Having lost the case, the Catholics were obliged to pay the court costs, a sum of $18,000. And this for a little wooden church which, together with its belltower, was hardly worth $1,000.

While all this passionate in-fighting was taking place at Star, Bishop Legal was growing ever more alarmed to see Orthodox missionaries making such inroads among the Ukrainian Catholic population. The Roman Catholic Church would stand by no longer. A series of official delegations were hurriedly dispatched to Rome and to Lviv. As a result, three Ukrainian Catholic priests, members of the Basilian Order, and four nuns, Sister Servants, arrived in Edmonton in 1902. They headed for the region most densely populated by Ukrainian homesteaders, and established a centre for their mission work in Mundare. In 1903 two more priests came to Canada, and settled in Manitoba. In time, this first contingent of Basilians was joined by a few more immigrant priests from Ukraine, and a group of French-speaking Belgian priests who took on the Eastern rite and learned the Ukrainian language so as to minister to the needy settlers.

This tiny handful of Ukrainian Catholic priests was faced with an enormous task and one that had to be carried out under the most adverse conditions. Their congregations were scattered over a vast and wild terrain. Much of the priests' time was spent travelling, yet there were no roads linking one colony to another. Until churches were built, the services were held in farmhouses. The people couldn't afford to maintain their priests in comfort. There were the harsh climate and physical dangers to contend with.

This demanding lifestyle took its toll in health and in lives. Father John Chrysostom Tymochko came to Canada in 1905. On a frigid winter day, December 19, 1909, he travelled twenty-five miles from Mundare to Wostok to say Mass. Father Tymochko's health was poor − he suffered from asthma − and the journey back proved too much for him. Upon his return to the mission centre he was found frozen to death on his sleigh.

The permanent presence of Ukrainian Catholic clergy in Canada boosted the morale of the Catholic immigrants considerably. At last, the continuation of their spiritual life was assured. But this wasn't enough to put an end to the religious troubles that plagued the Ukrainian community. For one thing, there were still no Ukrainian Orthodox priests to serve the Orthodox immigrants from Bukovina. Not all were content to live under the religious rule of Moscow. For another, a number of Catholics, still displeased with their Church's close ties with Roman Catholicism in the matter of church property, continued to defect from the ranks. The dissidents went in several directions: Some embraced Russian Orthodoxy; others joined the short-lived "Independent Greek Church" autonomous of both Rome and Moscow — which was established in Winnipeg by the self-proclaimed "Bishop" Seraphim Ustovolsky; a small number opted for Protestant faiths.

Hatred and suspicion continued to smoulder, most markedly in Alberta, where the conversion of Catholics to Russian Orthodoxy, and its resultant ill will and divisiveness, was most common. In a few communities, feelings ran so high they sometimes erupted into violence. Even allowing for the fact that the churches of that time were frail wooden structures, highly susceptible to fires begun by candles carelessly left burning, or bolts of lightning striking domes, an inordinate number of churches burned down. In 1910, following the unfortunate example of their compatriots at Star, the residents of three other Alberta colonies — Chipman, Rabbit Hill and Buford — fought legal battles over the ownership of their churches. Again, in all three cases, the Orthodox congregations were the victors.

In those regions where it was most intense, the bickering and strife not only sapped the colonies of their moral and financial resources, but destroyed the solidarity that would have enabled all Ukrainian immigrants to pull together towards common social, political and cultural goals.

After the First World War, Ukrainian religious life in emigration, so chaotic in its first years, began slowly to stabilize. The Ukrainian Catholic Church was establishing itself firmly on Canadian ground. The Russian mission, on the other hand, fell into a decline. The Russian revolution of 1917, which abolished the monarchy and the power of the Church in that country, deprived the mission of its source of funds. Without an influx of money, it soon lost its momentum. Those Ukrainian Orthodox settlers who had long hoped for a church organization independent of Moscow now went into action. In 1918 the Ukrainian Orthodox Brotherhood was founded in Saskatoon. That same year, three formerly Russian Orthodox congregations in Alberta joined the new movement. From that time it continued to gain ground in all three provinces, taking into its fold the majority of Orthodox churches in Ukrainian colonies. Only a small number chose to remain under Russian authority.

Nevertheless, in spite of quarrels, in areas outside the major battle zones the settlers led their religious lives in relative peace. The members of each church continued to practice their faith devoutly, as they had always done: they attended Mass on Sundays, blessed their Easter food and celebrated Christmas in the age-old traditional way. Once each colony was assured a regular visit from a priest every three or four weeks, churches began to go up thick and fast. Since a journey of even a few miles was a considerable undertaking, each tiny community erected a church of its own. Where there were residents of more than one faith, two or three churches went up. In the more densely populated regions, a traveller could hardly go more than four or five miles without seeing a church dome, topped with a cross, peering out from amongst the trees.

Building the First Churches

(opposite left)
The Shandro district of Alberta attracted a large number of settlers, many of them former residents of the village of Ruskiy-Banyliw in Bukovina. By 1902 the community was big enough to warrant a church of its own. Under the leadership of Nikon Shandro, a church building was organized. Only the chief builder, a man who had been a carpenter in his home village, was paid for his labour. He received the princely sum of $1 per day for working from dawn until dark. All the other settlers donated their time and their labour. The Shandro church took two years to complete.

(opposite right)
One of the most impressive churches in rural Alberta is St. Peter and Paul's Orthodox Church at Wastao. The church is sixty-five feet high. It stands on a hill, towering majestically over the fields and woods that surround it. Its builder, Stephan Rosichuk, was not an

No Ukrainian village was without its church. It dominated the village landscape; every peasant family lived within its sight. The church had stood in the same spot for decades, often for centuries. It embodied all that was most certain and immutable in the lives of the villagers: deep religious faith, tradition, stability.

In the parklands of western Canada, there were no villages, no churches, only an endless stretch of forests unmarked by human habitation: a strange and uncomfortable emptiness that the settlers longed to fill with familiar objects. Of these, the most important was the church. Its mere presence reassured the immigrants and made the new-country wilderness feel more like home.

The settlers had no money to buy elaborate building materials for their churches, or to hire craftsmen to conceive and construct them. In the colonies there were no architects, no master builders, not even many carpenters whose skills stretched beyond the building of houses and the fashioning of plain, homely furniture and farm tools. As a result, the churches in the new Ukrainian settlements, built by the settlers themselves under the direction of their most experienced carpenters, were small and modest structures, a far cry from the beautifully crafted, elaborately decorated church buildings that graced even the humblest Ukrainian village. But even these simple rural churches retained the essential features of the traditional Byzantine architectural style: round domes adorned with crosses, arched windows and doors, and, on the inside, ikons, and an ikonostasis that separated the altar from the main body of the church.

architect, but an illiterate immigrant from the village of Shepintsi, Bukovina. Although he could neither read nor write, this man was capable of recalling a church he had seen in his native province, visualizing the plan and reproducing it in the Alberta wilderness.

The church is a solid structure, built entirely of hand-hewn logs that were dragged by oxen from a nearby wood. Stephan Rosichuk and his helpers worked on the church for three years. It was begun in 1909, completed in 1912.

Religious Celebrations

The Ukrainian immigrants brought with them a host of religious customs and traditions which they followed as assiduously in Canada as they had back home. The Church calendar was a strong regulating force in their lives: it told them when to work and when to rest; when to do penance and when to celebrate. All religious regulations — both those set down by Church law and those that stemmed from folk tradition — were carried out scrupulously and to the letter.

On the pioneer homestead, the Lord's Day was indeed kept holy. When a priest came to the local church, the little building was crowded to overflowing. No member of the community failed to attend the service. Sunday was ordained a day of complete rest. Even in the busiest of seasons, at seeding and harvest time, to work in the fields would be unthinkable. Except for feeding and watering the livestock, no farm chores or household work was done. Even cutting with a knife was frowned upon.

Pearl Strynadka   On Sundays we didn't do anything in the house. We wouldn't sweep or wash anything. I used to hate Mondays! There would always be a big pile of dishes left from Sunday that I had to wash.

(above left)
The interior of St. Peter and
Paul's Orthodox Church at
Wastao.
(above right)
The all-seeing "eye of God"
looks down from the
ceiling of St. Onufrey's
Catholic Church. The
church, located a few miles
north of Smoky Lake, was
built in 1910.

(right)
A typical ikonostasis inside
a Ukrainian church. This
one is in Holy Ascension
Orthodox Church in Smoky
Lake.

Fasts were frequent and strictly observed. For a full seven weeks before Easter, the settlers denied themselves not only meat, but eggs, cheese, milk and butter too. Shorter periods of fast were prescribed before Christmas and major saints' days, the feasts of St. Peter and Paul (July 12), and the Virgin Mary (August 28). Every Friday of the year was a day of abstinence.

Some of the settlers who were particularly given to religious devotion — and these were most often women — carried out their religious observances with even more stringency and fervour than was required.

Mrs. Kowalchuk Every Sunday my mother would get up before sunrise. Until ten o'clock she would be on her knees, praying. During all that time we weren't allowed to eat anything. We children used to get so hungry waiting for her to finish her prayers. And when a priest came to our church, she never let us eat anything until we came home from the service. She believed it was a sin to ride to church. Even when she was old she would never ride in a wagon with her children. She still walked the two miles to the church.

Pearl Strynadka Many people were so religious in those days! My mother was like that. One summer she was expecting a baby. Well, for two weeks before August 28th was a fast. So even though her baby was coming soon, my mother kept that fast. She wouldn't even drink milk during that time.

The steadfast adherence to their familiar religious practices brought spiritual comfort to the settlers, but it did even more than that. It gave them a sense of stability and continuity as they made the transition from life in the Old Country to the new. And, it served a practical purpose, too, ensuring that the overworked homesteaders put away their ploughs and their spindles for at least one day out of seven.

Christmas Even on the homestead the daily routine sometimes gave way to joy and celebration. During the major religious festivals the settlers put aside all thoughts of work, all worries about the future, and absorbed themselves in re-enacting, in their new environment, the same traditional rituals and ceremonies that had been played and re-played for untold centuries in villages across Ukraine.

There was no time more festive than the Christmas season, which together with the New Year and the Epiphany, lasted for a period of two weeks. Christmas meant feasts and carols, joyful family visits and special religious services. Interwoven with the purely religious aspects of the commemoration of the birth of Christ were a multitude of rituals that derived from ancient pre-Christian sources and

At the centre of the Christmas table stood a pair of braided loaves, or *kolachi*. A candle was placed inside the bread. The loaves remained on the table for the duration of the Christmas season.

were primarily agricultural in nature. During the holiday season farmers took care to do all those things which, they hoped, would entice whimsical fate into being kind to them during the year to come, and into granting them productivity in the fields, the garden and the stables.

Ukrainian Church holidays were celebrated according to the Julian calendar which, several centuries ago, had been supplanted in the West by the newer Gregorian calendar. Because of the thirteen day difference in calculation between the two calendars, Ukrainian Christmas fell on January 7th. The first, and the most celebrated day of the Christmas season was Christmas Eve, January 6th.

Christmas Eve was a day of strict fast; the settlers took no solid food until early evening. Then, an elaborate meal of twelve traditional meatless dishes marked the beginning of the Christmas celebrations. The early part of the day was a busy time on the homestead, a time of preparation for the festive season ahead. Everything had to be finished and in its place by suppertime, for once the holiday period began all work would cease. From dawn until sunset a fire blazed in the kitchen stove, as the mother of the family put her best culinary talents to work, mixing and kneading, cooking, frying and baking the complicated array of food she would serve for the evening meal. In the meantime, the father bustled around the farm, attending to last-minute chores. He took extra pains to ensure that all the animals were comfortable and well fed, for on this special night of the year, according to ancient legend, animals were gifted with the power of human speech, and would complain to God if they were maltreated by their owners.

The children scurried around the house and farm assisting their parents, but their chief preoccupation was the impending Christmas Eve supper, a once-a-year treat they anticipated with great relish. Late in the afternoon they hung about the farmyard, waiting for the first star – the Star of Bethlehem – to appear in the winter sky. As soon as it was sighted, the meal could begin.

The main room of the house was decorated to suit the occasion in a manner prescribed by tradition. In one corner of the room stood a sheaf of wheat. A layer of loose hay covered the table, under the tablecloth. Below the table, more hay was scattered on the floor, and on it lay a few common farm tools – a sickle, a whetstone, a hammer, perhaps a ploughshare – symbols of the agricultural life of the people. A place was set for every member of the family, including those who were absent: if they couldn't be present in person, they would at least be there in spirit. In the middle of the table sat two round braided loaves of bread, or *kolachi*. In the hole in their centre stood a glass of salt, and in the salt, a candle.

As the evening fell, the family gathered around the table, each person in his proper place. Candles were lit. The father led his family in prayer. The mother waved incense over the food, then placed it aside to burn for the duration of the meal.

Supper began with *kutia*, a special sweet dish of boiled wheat, poppy seeds and honey, made only at Christmas-time. Before dishing it out to his children, the father threw a spoonful up to the ceiling to bring good luck and an abundant harvest in the coming year. An assortment of succulent dishes followed the *kutia*: borshch with mushroom-filled dumplings, fish, two kinds of pyrohy, holubtsi, cornmeal, various vegetables, mushrooms, cooked dried fruit and sweet buns.

When the meal was over, the dishes were cleared away, except for the *kutia* and the *kolachi*, which remained in their place on the table for the whole of the Christmas season. The entire family joined together in singing Christmas carols. Sometime during the evening, a group of carollers from the church came to the farm. They sang to the family, wished them good health and good fortune, and stayed long enough to enjoy a taste of the Christmas Eve meal and a drink or two. Some of the leftover food was made up into a bundle for the children to carry to a relative or a less fortunate neighbour. The night was well advanced by the time the happy, tired celebrants went to sleep.

Christmas Day, the first of three days of Christmas, began with an early service at the local church. Then the feasting and the carolling continued. The second and third days of Christmas were given over to visiting. The long distance between homesteads and the bone chilling cold that regularly blanketed the prairie provinces in January, didn't keep the settlers from hitching up their sleighs and driving out to share their merriment with friends and family.

New Year No sooner did the Christmas festivities wind down than it came time to celebrate again, to welcome the arrival of the New Year. New Year's Day fell a week after Christmas, on January 14th of the Gregorian calendar. Tradition demanded that the New Year be rung in on a note of merriment. New Year's Eve, known popularly as Malanka, was a night for carefree celebration, for dancing, singing, masquerade and trickery.

The young men of each district gathered together in the evening to organize a travelling masquerade party. Odd bits of clothing were transformed into costumes representing traditional Malanka characters. There might be an old couple, a young one, a policeman, a Jew, a fortune-telling Gypsy, a hideous devil and maybe a goat, dressed up in a sheepskin coat turned fur side out. This cast of characters, accompanied by a musician playing a violin, made the rounds of the homesteads in their area. At each house they visited, the Malanka party performed a little dance, sang songs, told jokes to their hosts and played tricks on the little children who peered fearfully at the wondrous visitors from behind their mother's skirts. In return for the entertainment, the hosts plied the young men with food and drink, and, if they could, slipped them a few coins. The party continued until the early hours of the morning.

On New Year's Day the settlers stayed at home. Much of the day was passed in fortune-telling and divination. The settlers performed rituals designed to predict and favourably influence the productivity of their farm during the following summer.

The previous night, just before she went to bed, the mother of the family had put lumps of charcoal on the stove, one lump for each type of crop grown on the farm. Now the family looked to see how the charcoal had fared overnight. If they found the lumps burned white, ready to fall apart at the touch, they could rest assured that their crops would be abundant. But if the charcoal remained black, still in solid lumps, the outlook for the harvest was poor.

In the afternoon, the children gathered a few grain seeds from the barn, brought them into the house, and walked from room to room, pretending to sow. To ensure fertility among the animals as well, they brought with them a small animal, a calf or a lamb. First they performed these rituals in their own home, then they went on to do the same in the houses of nearby neighbours.

Jordan The third and final major holiday of the Christmas season was the Epiphany, or, as it was known in the Ukrainian Church, the Feast of the River Jordan. This holiday fell on January 19th. The evening before Jordan, *Shchedrey Vechir,* or "Generous Eve," was celebrated as a second Christmas Eve. Once again the family sat down to a traditional festive meal, a less elaborate version of the one they ate on Christmas Eve. As a reminder of Christ's baptism in the River Jordan, the settlers adorned all the doorways of their house with crosses fashioned out of dough or wax. After supper the family sang *shchedrivky*, carols peculiar to this holiday.

Jordan itself was celebrated with the blessing of water at the river or creek that lay nearest to the church. A day or two in advance of the feast, the men of the parish erected a tall ice cross on the river's edge in preparation for the water-blessing ceremony. Almost without fail, January 19th dawned as one of the coldest days of the western Canadian winter. Temperatures of thirty or forty degrees below zero weren't abnormal. But mere cold, no matter how intense, couldn't keep the settlers in their houses on this day. Come what may, they would get their supply of holy water. Bundled up in heavy sheepskin coats, their heads wrapped in thick woolen shawls or covered tightly with fur caps pulled down over their ears, all the parishioners of the rural church marched in solemn procession from the church building to the river, carrying banners and singing as they walked. The crowd stood by patiently in the cold while the priest blessed the river water. Each member of the congregation clutched a jar or a pitcher, which he filled with holy water as soon as the service was over. At home, each member of the family drank a glass of the blessed water. The rest was stored away to be used as needed in the following year as protection against evil and danger. It would be sprinkled around the house during severe thunderstorms, and given to drink to family members who fell ill.

With Jordan, the Christmas holiday season drew to a close. The following day, the wheat sheaf and the hay that had decorated the house since Christmas Eve were taken out and burned. Women resumed their spinning, and, a few days later, their washing. Men returned to their heavy farm chores. The work-a-day routine of homestead life fell upon the settlers once more.

Easter   One immigrant, having just experienced his first Easter in Canada, was moved to express his disappointment in a poem:

Marunchak, p. 298.   *Our Easter is so beautiful,*
As the green grove,
While here in Canada —snow and ice,
And cold winds blow.

It was true, Easter on the homestead lacked the springtime charm and beauty of Easter in the Ukrainian village. By the computation of the Julian calendar, the date of Easter Sunday ranged from the same day as, to five weeks later than, the Gregorian Easter. But even in years when the holiday fell in late April or early May, it still found western Canadian nature unprepared for a festival of spring rebirth. The days were still cold. The trees were still bare. There was not a flower in sight. At this time of year more than any other the immigrants were prone to feeling twinges of nostalgia as, in their bleak and barren surroundings, they reviewed in their minds scenes from Easters past: neat white village houses shining in the sun, green meadows, fragrant blossoming trees.

But the cheerless Canadian climate didn't cool the settlers' ardour in celebrating their traditional Easter customs. Far in advance of the festival, they began their preparations with a prolonged period of penance and austerity, a seven-week fast during which they touched no meat, animal fats, eggs or dairy products. At the outset of Lent, the conscientious farmwife scrubbed out all her pots and pans to remove every trace of accumulated grease. She would let none of the forbidden foods creep into her family's diet. Lenten meals relied heavily on fish, vegetables, a good supply of hemp and poppy oil and bread baked without milk or eggs.

Eastertime began in earnest one week before Easter, on Palm Sunday. On this day willow branches were blessed in church. Every member of the congregation carried a blessed branch home. On Monday, the solemn Passion Week began. The early part of the week passed in a flurry of housecleaning, cooking and baking. Everything in the home had to be fresh and clean for Easter. There were sweet cakes (*babka*) to be baked, and a special Easter bread (*paska*), a large, round loaf fancifully decorated with braids, circles and crosses shaped out of dough. There was a rush to complete all the demanding farm chores too, for from Thursday evening on no heavy work would be permitted.

The best part of the Easter preparations was the decoration of Easter eggs, or *pysanky*. On Monday or Tuesday of Holy Week, the farmwife gathered fresh eggs from her henhouse, picking out the most perfectly shaped, and cooked them. At a table laid out with the tools of her craft — eggs, bowls of dyes, beeswax, a stylus — she sat down to the delicate, painstaking task of covering the eggs with intricate, multicoloured decorations. She reproduced traditional, regional designs from memory, or copied them from bits of eggshell kept from the previous year. The artistically gifted woman gave full vent to her creativity, improvising an endless variety of new designs based on those she had learned in the past. The less talented simply copied pre-established patterns. But whatever her abilities, no woman failed to make *pysanky*. Her daughters sat with her, slowly learning the skill for themselves. The younger ones worked clumsily, spoiling more eggs than they completed. It was no easy exercise to draw neat, straight, even lines on the curved surface of an egg. Children who weren't capable of producing a *pysanka* amused themselves with colouring the more simple *krashanky*, eggs that were dyed one solid colour.

All the egg decorating had to be finished by the afternoon of Holy Thursday, for folk custom held that any eggs produced after Christ's Passion had begun would turn to stone. Thursday evening was marked by a mournful church service commemorating Christ's suffering in the Garden. Good Friday, the day of the Crucifixion, was the most solemn day in the Church calendar. Signs of mourning were everywhere. People dressed themselves in their darkest clothing to attend the Good Friday service. The church was draped with black cloth. Bells were silenced; their ringing tone was replaced by the dull sound of wooden clappers. An image of the dead Christ lay in the front of the church. At the end of the service it was carried in procession three times around the church. Good Friday was a day of strictest fast, from which only children, the feeble and the very old were exempt. No food at all was taken by the faithful. The very religious extended the fast even longer, some choosing to abstain from all food from the evening of Holy Thursday until after Easter Mass on Sunday.

Easter Sunday ended this long period of mourning and privation. At dawn, bells began to peal, proclaiming the news of Christ's resurrection. The settlers hurried to church, this time all dressed in their finest apparel. Each family carried a big basket filled with traditional Easter food. Once the long Easter Mass was finished, the parishioners stood in a ring around the church, their baskets on the ground before them, opened to reveal their contents: *paska* (Easter bread), *babka* (sweet cake), eggs, sausage, ham, cheese, butter, lard, horseradish, garlic, salt and pepper and of course, *pysanky* and *krashanky*. The priest walked around the circle, blessing each basket. People parted from each other in the churchyard with much well-wishing, and hurried home with their baskets to partake of the blessed food, their first non-Lenten meal in many weeks.

Like Christmas, Easter lasted a full three days. No work was done in this time. The settlers gathered together in the churchyard or in each others' homes to exchange Easter greetings, eat, sing, trade *pysanky* and celebrate the promised arrival of the new spring season.

Ukrainian Hutzul legend,
Nadia Odette Diakun,
Women's World, May 1975, no. 5, p. 19.

The fate of the world depends upon the *pysanka*. As long as the tradition of decorating eggs with brilliant colours at Eastertide remains and is passed from one generation to the next, the world will continue to exist. Should the custom cease or be destroyed, evil will encompass and destroy the world. Evil — is a horrid monstrous creature chained to the side of a jagged cliff. Each year the advocates of the villain record the number of *pysanky* decorated. The greater the number — the tighter the chains hold the creature; but once the number of *pysanky* is decreased, the links loosen and the creature's strength begins to build.

Pysanky

The practice of decorating eggs is deeply rooted in Ukrainian folk life. Its origins pre-date recorded history. With the advent of Christianity in Ukraine, this widespread folk custom was incorporated into the celebration of Easter. The egg, always a symbol of eternity, now took on a Christian significance as a sign of eternal life.

Pysanka designs vary from one region to the next, but all are basically composed of geometric patterns and highly stylized nature motifs. The most commonly used design elements are geometric patterns: thin lines, both straight and wavy, and wide belts that divide the egg into several parts, triangles and pointed star shapes. Plant motifs also appear regularly. These are far more often depicted in a stylized than in a realistic form. Pine branches, oak leaves, and simplified flowers — roses, periwinkles, sunflowers — are the most popular plant designs. Human figures are never used, but in some regions of Ukraine various animals — reindeer, horses, fish and roosters — crop up in the design. In addition to the basic geometric, plant and animal motifs, *pysanka* makers make use of many decorative touches, whose function is to fill out the design. These decorative elements take the shape of little nets or gratings, dots and spirals.

All major *pysanka* motifs have a symbolic meaning, many dating back to antiquity. A large number of the oldest designs are symbols of

the sun. The sun appears on the egg in the form of circles, stars, rosettes and tripods. Triangles represent a triad. Formerly used to signify a triad of natural forces — air, fire and water, the triangle has come, in recent times, to be a symbol of the Trinity. The endless line or belt is a sign of eternity. Some designs — crosses, fish, little churches — have a purely Christian significance.

Pysanky are coloured according to the batik technique. The *pysanka* maker begins with a white egg. She dips her wire stylus into melted beeswax and covers with the wax all parts of the egg that are to remain white in the final pattern. Then she dips the egg into a bowl of yellow dye. The dye must be cold; if it were hot, the wax would melt. Except for the waxed-off portions, the egg is now yellow. The *pysanka* maker applies a coat of wax where she wants the design to be yellow, then dips the egg into orange dye. She proceeds in the same manner through red, and finally to the darkest colour, black or a deep wine. If she intends to dye any part of the egg green or blue, colours that don't fit into the main tonal range, she must apply these colours separately, after the waxing process is complete.

Once the whole design has been applied, the *pysanka* maker places the egg inside a warm oven or holds it over a candle flame. The wax melts away to reveal the pattern in its full range of colours.

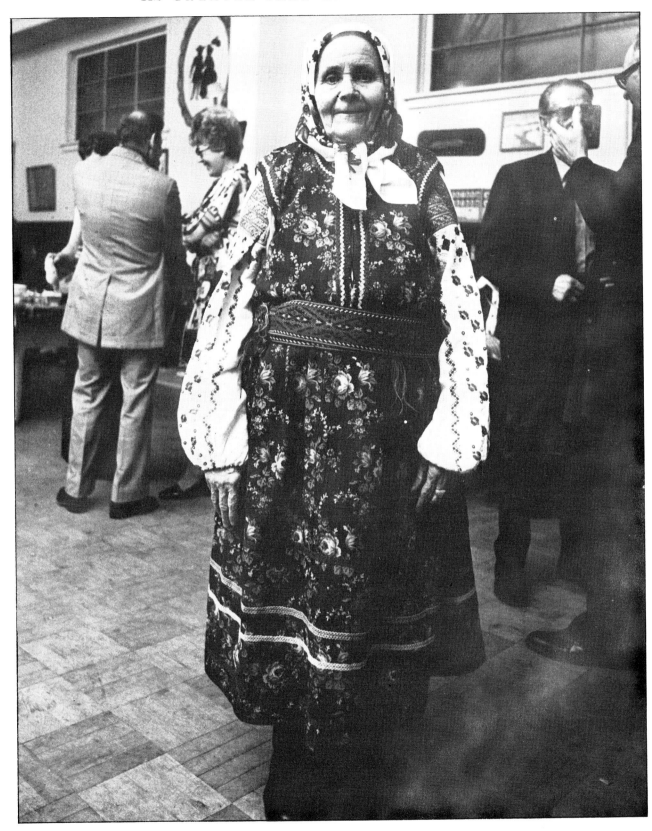

5 The Years That Followed

Czumer, p. 161, (author's translation).

The role played by Ukrainian settlers in Canada deserves serious attention. The Ukrainians came here with only the ten fingers on their hands — they had no other possessions. And within fifty years of their arrival, they were able to point proudly to great achievements. Success didn't come to them easily; it required great effort and hard work. For what was their role at that time if not that of the lowly labourer — the cultivator of wild western soil . . . ?

Central and Eastern Europeans were brought to Canada only when it became clear that other settlers would be unable to win the Great West. They were brought in like shock troops in a war, the last forces sent in to break through heavily defended battle lines and to take by force enemy-held territories. They were brought in like those African slaves of the seventeenth and eighteenth centuries who were sent into the southern United States in order to create there enormous plantations of cotton, tobacco and corn. In the dense forests and wide plains of Western Canada at the turn of the twentieth century, the Ukrainian colonists fulfilled a similar function. Their role was to succeed or to perish. And they threw themselves vigorously into the conquest of the western Canadian wilderness, transforming it in time into the fertile fields that today we sow with golden wheat and a variety of other rich crops.

Victoria Zaharia, Smoky Lake, Alberta.

The Interwar Years

The summer of 1914 brought an abrupt stop to the steady influx into the West of Central and Eastern Europeans. The Great War broke out. Canada and Austria became enemy countries. For the duration of the war, Canada's doors slammed shut to citizens of Austrian-held territories.

This was the end of the first and most significant wave of Ukrainian emigration into Canada. Over the next four decades, Ukrainians would continue to trickle in, but never again would they come in such huge numbers. While 200,000 came in prior to World War I, only 70,000 arrived in the years between the wars, and 30,000 after World War II. And never again would newcomers face conditions as primitive and inhospitable as those encountered by the pioneer immigrants.

The first great push to open Canada's west was already over by the end of the First World War. Now the challenge was of a different order: not to begin development, but to enlarge and to expand.

The original pioneer settlers and their children carried on their work on the land. Poverty-stricken homesteaders of twenty years earlier were beginning to make remarkable gains. Not all settlers progressed as speedily as the farmers in the fertile region around Shandro, Alberta, but their impressive growth is indicative of the general improvement in the position of Ukrainian immigrants. This is how the farmers of Shandro stood in 1929:

Marunchak, p. 353.

average number of years here: 27
average land holdings: 2.6 quarter sections
average clearing per farm: 248 acres

The rapid progress of the Shandro settlers, who only a few years earlier were straining to hack out one or two acres of land per year, was due almost entirely to one factor: increased mechanization. Ukrainian farmers didn't hesitate to follow the example of their English-speaking neighbours in adopting more efficient farming methods. Every spare dollar went to pay for improved agricultural equipment. The old-world sickles and scythes — tools that sufficed for miniscule old-country plots of land, but were inadequate in the enormous expanses of western Canada — were fast disappearing. Plodding oxen were traded in for teams of horses; in a short time, the horses, too, would yield their place to the more powerful and efficient tractors and trucks.

Small towns were springing up in the Ukrainian colonies, to serve as supply and grain-delivery centres for the farmers in each district. Like most small prairie towns, Smoky Lake grew up where it did because of its location on a railway line, which came through the area in 1919. Lying in the heart of a region populated by Ukrainians, the town's store signs are bilingual. The trade that went on inside the shops would have been conducted almost totally in Ukrainian.

Confident-looking young people, all dressed in their finest Canadian apparel, ride to church, Easter, 1924.

A group of neat, well-scrubbed Ukrainian children, students at a Protestant mission school in Smoky Lake, late 1920s. Nothing about their appearance speaks of their "foreign" origin.

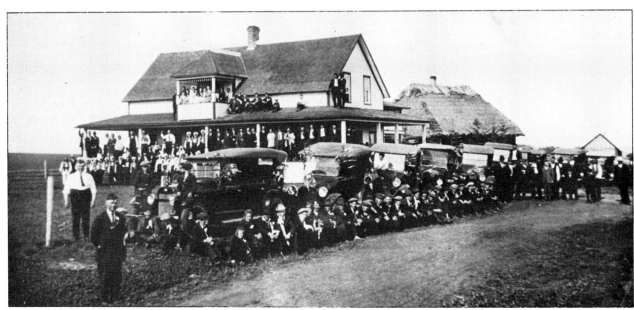

The single ox that pulled ploughs and harrows during the pioneer era has given way to a team of four horses on this Alberta farm, photographed in 1940. This land was once nothing but marsh and bush. Now it stands wide open, and is sown with a rich crop of grain, thanks to the efforts of the Ukrainian family that settled it thirty years earlier.

Even these horses have almost come to the end of their time. During the early 1940s, western farmers were mechanizing their operations at a rapid rate. In 1941 farmers in Alberta already owned 25,000 tractors, 3,000 combines, 40,000 cars and 8,000 trucks.

This wedding reception held at a farm near Shandro in 1926, shows a blend of the old and the new. The bride standing on the upper balcony is dressed in white. The older women, below, still wear traditional garb. The line of cars parked in the yard tells of a new prosperity. The farmhouse is roomy and modern. Behind it, the family's first house, thatched and whitewashed, stands as a reminder of earlier, leaner years.

The increased use of power other than their own arms and their own backs enabled the Ukrainian settlers to speed up dramatically the work of clearing and breaking land. It enabled them to finish clearing their homesteads — those first quarter sections that had once appeared so vast, and even to begin extending their holdings by buying up neighbouring quarter sections.

During the interwar years the fortunes of the Ukrainian settlers waxed and waned in the same way as those of all western Canadian farmers. In the 1920s they progressed, and experienced a moderate prosperity. With the 1930s came the Depression, and ten years of privation. Having just attained a modicum of security, the settlers now saw their work go to nothing. Prices for their hard-won produce slipped to rock-bottom levels: wheat to 12 - 18c per bushel, eggs to 4c per dozen, beef to 1c per pound, live weight, and pork to 2 - 4c per pound. The average income of farmers had been $791 per annum in the late 1920s; during the 1930s, it dropped to $329. In the 1940s, their lot improved once more. The war drove prices upward. But it also took their sons, along with other young Canadian men, into battle overseas.

Throughout these years older settlers, those who had emigrated to Canada as adults, continued to cling to their native language, dress and customs. They were too old to change. But the younger generation, those born, or at least raised in Canada, were beginning to cast off the marks of their origins. In a rush to become more "Canadian" — and thus more acceptable in the eyes of outsiders, the young were giving up Ukrainian dress, their parents' more extreme religious practices and, to some extent, their language. Out of shame over the scorn they evinced from Anglo-Canadians, many people burned their homespun clothing, or tore it up for rags. For some, Ukrainian was becoming not the first but a second tongue, reserved for conversing with parents and older relatives.

In part, these changes were motivated by the natural desire of a younger generation, more affluent and better educated than its parents, to progress and modernize. Peasant ways couldn't be maintained for long in a mechanized society which held no place for a peasant class. But the rush to abandon old ways was speeded on its way by the prejudice against Ukrainians that was still all too prevalent. Although newspapers no longer printed the vitriolic attacks on Ukrainians that filled their pages in former years, the view that Slavs were inferior and backward people hadn't yet lost currency.

Individual cases of prejudice weren't uncommon. Pioneer teacher W. Czumer recounts one such incident that was widely reported in the press in 1941:

Czumer, 149-50,
(author's translation).

The school board of the district of Hampton, five miles from Bowmanville, Ontario, hired a talented nineteen-year-old teacher, Maria Kozak, to teach in the local school. But someone in the district took exception to Miss Kozak's foreign name and her parents' foreign background, and went out among the taxpayers collecting signatures to block her appointment. Ninety taxpayers out of one hundred agreed to sign their names to a petition demanding that the local trustees not accept Miss Kozak into their school.

Miss Kozak had already signed a contract, so she asked for damages to which she was entitled according to the agreement. Although the school district was obliged to pay her $180 in costs, the English "patriots" of Hampton, Ontario had their way and succeeded in keeping Miss Kozak out of their school.

By 1941 Ukrainians had been in Canada for fifty years, but still a Ukrainian name could be a liability. It is no wonder, then, that during the 1930s and 1940s, a sizeable number of Ukrainians anglicized their names, and not a few abandoned the church of their parents in favour of Roman Catholicism or Protestantism.

Throughout the interwar years, assimilation was the order of the day. It was held without question that immigrants must be assimilated as quickly and as completely as possible. In schools across the West, children of immigrants were instructed in English only, and were well grounded in the basic principles of the Canadian way of life. As one Alberta school official reported optimistically in 1930:

Inspector Owen Williams,
25th Annual Report of the Department of Education of the Province of Alberta, 1930. Edmonton: King's Printer, 1931, p. 60.

The data on New Canadian schools are very encouraging. It is direct proof that our efforts at assimilation are meeting with success. By the time the third generation reaches adolescence, the distinction of language, culture and customs will have disappeared, so that a visitor to these parts will not be able to tell where the so-called foreign belt starts.

Educators like Mr. Williams hoped that these schoolchildren would soon give up their native language and cease to identify with the mother country of their parents. Mr. Williams' vision of a homogeneously Anglo-Saxon western Canada did not come to pass, but the winds of change were beginning to blow through the Ukrainian colonies.

Still, the change couldn't be described as wholesale assimilation. Even as they wore modern dress and spoke fluent English, most Ukrainians still remained Ukrainian. On the whole, they assimilated far less rapidly than most Western Europeans. For a number of reasons, Ukrainians continued to identify strongly with their cultural roots: because they were more "foreign" to begin with, and thus had

A family gathering at Shandro, Alberta, 1930s.

a greater barrier of prejudice to overcome; because the hold of centuries of peasant tradition, which had withstood all efforts by outside powers to destroy it, was too strong to be abandoned lightly; because the presence of old people and new Ukrainian immigrants kept the language and customs alive; and because, for the most part, the people were still living on the land, in relative isolation.

During the period between the two wars, the majority of Ukrainians in Canada lived and worked on farms. Census figures from this era show that rural dwellers by far outnumbered urban dwellers. Taking into account that many of the urban Ukrainians were new immigrants who chose to remain in large centres where work was available, it becomes clear that by and large, the Ukrainians remained an agricultural people.

Marunchak, p. 351.

Canadians of Ukrainian Origin

Year	Per cent Rural	Per cent Urban
1911	85	15
1921	80	20
1931	70	30
1941	66	34

Dr. C.H. Andrusyshen;

P. J. Lazarowich, "Ukrainian Pioneers in Western Canada", *Alberta Historial Review 5*, 5 (Autumn, 1957), p. 20.

According to one western authority:

The general development of the Canadian West and more specifically the development of Canadian agriculture was their greatest single contribution to the culture of this country. . . . We may safely say that forty percent of all the wheat growing land in Western Canada was brought under cultivation by Ukrainian farmers.

What Remains

Prof. W.L. Morgan,
Winnipeg, 1951;
Lazarowich, p. 27.

(top left and right)
The violin and the
dulcimer were the
favourite folk instruments
of the pioneer settlers. And
they are still popular today.
Bands that play Ukrainian
folk music provide
entertainment at dances
and at weddings. The
dulcimer has to be made by
hand. In every region there
is still someone who knows
how to make them.

The most important folk
customs associated with
the major religious
holidays are still kept alive
by Ukrainian Canadians. At
Easter, women still
decorate eggs, bake paska
and carry baskets of food to
church for blessing. At
Christmas they still
prepare a supper of twelve
meatless dishes.
(bottom left)
Anastasia Zazula prepares
a traditional Christmas Eve
supper in her home at
Shandro. She waves
incense over the food
before the meal begins.
(bottom right)
Blessing the Easter paska at
the Ukrainian Orthodox
church in Willingdon,
Alberta.

In entering into the common heritage, the Ukrainian pioneers brought much: love of the soil, a static and conservative factor in our dynamic society; folk culture, a vital source for the arts in music, painting, letters and the dance; passion for freedom, by which the democratic faith of this country has been revived and renewed; devotion to culture, by which the cultivation of learning and the arts has been refreshed and strengthened. It is a great accession to the common store, of which Ukrainian Canadians may be proud, and for which all Canadians are grateful.

The years that followed World War Two brought a growing recognition of Canada's cultural diversity and of her ''common heritage,'' a heritage shaped not only by French and Anglo-Canadians, but also by immigrants from a variety of national backgrounds. The experiences of the first generation of Ukrainian immigrants were now accorded their place in Canadian history. Their struggles were being recognized for their instrumental role in the development of the West; their cultural traditions accepted for having enriched the Canadian mosaic.

In the post-war period, western Canada underwent many changes: a total mechanization of agriculture, an enormous growth in the size of the family farm, and, simultaneously, a massive influx of population from the countryside to the cities. All these changes have altered the face of the Ukrainian population.

Today, Ukrainians, most of them descendants of pioneer settlers, form the third largest ethnic group in all three prairie provinces. They are no longer a group apart, living in isolation in rural colonies. The majority are urban dwellers and are engaged in every type of occupation; all are fully integrated into Canadian society. The social progress of Ukrainians has been rapid; innumerable grandchildren of illiterate immigrants occupy positions in universities, the professions and government.

Pressure on Ukrainians to conform to the Anglo-Canadian norm, at the expense of their own mother culture, has subsided in recent years. The policy of total assimilation, once fervently espoused on official levels, has been supplanted by the more tolerant attitude embodied in the policy of multiculturalism. The Ukrainian customs and traditions that are still maintained by the third and fourth generation — language, religion and folk arts — have ceased to be objects of derision. They are even acclaimed as a vital part of the Canadian identity.

Plastered houses are still a common sight in the rural regions that were first settled by Ukrainians. They stand desolate in open fields, their plaster peeling, their straw roofs long since rotted away. The houses are relics from an age when farmlands were densely populated. At one time, when landholdings were small, each quarter section of land was occupied by a different family. Today, one farmer owns several quarter sections; the houses on them have become superfluous. The depopulation of farmland has been dramatic. Near Smoky Lake, for example, a six mile square area of land held ninety-seven families in 1910. In 1973 the same area had only thirty families.

A demonstration of old-fashioned flailing. When Ukrainian immigrants came to Canada, they brought with them sickles and scythes. They made flails and rakes out of wood on the homestead. Since that time, agriculture has undergone a complete revolution. Hand tools, manual flour mills and walking ploughs sit useless and forgotten in museums. Only on special occasions are they brought out of storage. Then, old people who still remember recreate pioneer life for the young.

Faces of the Pioneers:
These people witnessed
the beginnings of
Ukrainian settlement in
Canada. Some emigrated as
youngsters; others were
born during the first years
of their parents' stay on the
homestead. These old
people lived in dugouts.
They went to work on
railroads. They cleared
land by hand. They knew
hunger and cold and
misery. And they saw the
West change from wild
frontier land to what it is
today.
(p. 164 clockwise from top
left)
Mr. Palamarek,
Waskatenau, Alberta.
Mrs. Socholototsky, Smoky
Lake, Alberta.
John Korol, Theodore,
Saskatchewan.
Steve Stogrin, Smoky Lake.
(p. 165 clockwise from top
left)
George Kowalchuk,
Willingdon, Alberta.
Anastasia Zazula,
Shandro, Alberta.
George Shewchuk,
Vegreville, Alberta.
Mary Starchuk, Smoky
Lake.

In this age of galloping technological advancement, extensive mobility and constantly shifting lifestyles, history moves at a fast pace. The first permanent white settlement of the Canadian West took place so recently that some of the early settlers are still alive, yet the pioneer era seems as remote from us today as a totally different world.

To the present-day city dweller, the farm tools and everyday objects used by his own grandparents are unrecognizable. The countryside he views from his car window tells him little of the past. Its stretches of open grainfields appear to have always been there: there is no sign of the human struggle that went into creating them.

But in those same regions of the western parklands that Ukrainian immigrants took as homesteads seventy or eighty years ago, some traces of the past remain. The land that was cleared by the first generation is worked today by the third or the fourth. On county maps in parkland regions, the names of landholders are still overwhelmingly Ukrainian — the same names as those of the original homesteaders. The small towns retain their Ukrainian character. Even today, Ukrainian vies with English as the dominant language in the stores and on the street. Every few miles along country roads there are round-domed churches. Some are still in use; others, locked up for good, are victims of a dwindling rural population and a less religious age. Old houses, the first homes of pioneer families, still stand in the fields. And there are the people — old people who lived through the pioneer era, and still remember.

Ukrainian immigrants came to Canada seeking a better life. Some thought they were coming to a Promised Land, and they were disappointed. But eventually most of their dreams were fulfilled. They came for land, and they got land, more than they ever imagined. They wanted freedom from wars and oppression, and a brighter future for their children. Today, their grandchildren live in peace, liberty and prosperity. It took many years, a great deal of work and much suffering, but the Ukrainian immigrants got from Canada what they wanted. At the same time, they gave it much more.

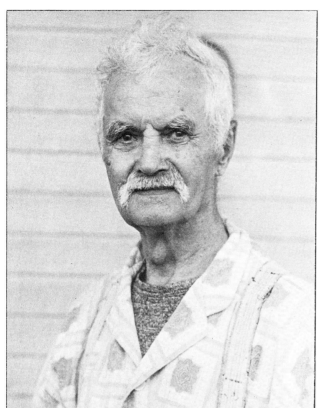

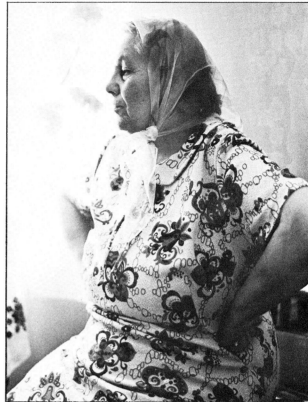

Chronology of Important Events in the First Years of Ukrainian Settlement in Canada

1891 September: The first two Ukrainians to come to Canada — Ivan Pylypiw and Vasyl Eleniak, from the village of Nebiliw in Galicia — arrive in Montreal. From there they travel west.

1892 Pylypiw returns to Nebiliw, while Eleniak remains in Canada. For disseminating information about Canadian homesteads, Pylypiw is arrested, charged with sedition and sent to prison. At the same time, twelve families from Nebiliw leave for Canada. Some of them go to Alberta, some stay in Winnipeg, others go to Gretna, Manitoba, to work for German farmers.

1892 — 94 The first Ukrainian colony in Canada springs up at Beaverhill Creek (also known as Edna, and later, Star), east of Edmonton. All the immigrants are former residents of Nebiliw.

1893 14 February: The first child of Ukrainian immigrant parents born on Canadian soil, in Winnipeg — Franko Yatsiw, son of Vasyl and Maria.
Spring: Pylypiw returns to Canada with his family. He goes to Bruderheim, Alberta, then takes a homestead at Edna/Star.

1895 Dr. Joseph Oleskiw tours Canada with an eye to resettling poor Ukrainian peasants in western Canada. He travels extensively through the West, and in August visits the Ukrainian colonists at Edna/Star. Upon his return to Galicia he publishes a book describing the new country.

1896 The Liberal government of Sir Wilfred Laurier accedes to power. In a drive to populate and develop the empty spaces of the Canadian West, the Laurier government extends its search for immigrants to Central Europe. Clifford Sifton is named Minister of the Interior and placed in charge of immigration matters.
"Emigration fever" spreads through Galicia and its neighbouring province, Bukovina. Ukrainians flock to Canada in ever-growing numbers.
The Canadian press begins to react to this massive influx of "non-preferred" Slavic immigrants. On **December 14** the *Edmonton Bulletin* states in an editorial, "They are not a people that are wanted in this country at any price." On **December 23** the Winnipeg *Daily Nor-Wester* proclaims, "The Southern Slavs are probably the least promising of all the material that could be selected for nation building."
Ukrainian colonies are formed in Manitoba, at Stuartburn, Gonor, Brokenhead and Dauphin.
The first Ukrainian colony springs up in southern Saskatchewan, near Grenfell. It does not last long, probably because of the lack of wood in this prairie region.
The first Ukrainian immigrant gets full title to land in Canada — Fedir Fuhr of Rabbit Hill, south of Edmonton.

1897 The first permanent Ukrainian colony is formed in Saskatchewan, in the area of Fish Creek and Crooked Lake, near the town of Wakaw.
September-October: For the first time since their arrival in Canada, Ukrainian settlers are visited by a priest of their rite. Father Nestor Dmytriw, a Ukrainian Catholic priest living in the USA, comes through Stuartburn and Edna/Star. At Star he founds the first Ukrainian Catholic parish in Canada.
Missionaries from the Russian Orthodox Church come to Edna/Star. The seeds are sown for a long and bitter conflict between Catholics and Orthodox in the community.

1898 The first Ukrainian church in Canada is built at Edna/Star.

1899 Clifford Sifton signs an immigrant-recruiting agreement with the North Atlantic Trading Co. The agreement is renewed in 1904.

Ukrainian settlers begin to organize school districts. The first is Galicia S.D. in Manitoba.

1901 During the celebration of Easter Mass, hostilities break out over the ownership of the Edna/Star church.

1902 **1 November:** Ukrainian priests take up permanent residence in Canada. A group of three Catholic priests of the Basilian order and four Sisters Servants of Mary Immaculate arrive at Strathcona, South Edmonton. In the group are Fathers Platonid Filas, Sozont Dydyk and Anton Strotsky, and Sisters Ambrosia, Taida, Emelia and Isidore.

1903 **15 November:** The first Ukrainian-language newspaper in Canada begins publication — the *Canadian Farmer*, edited in Winnipeg by Ivan Negrych.

1904 **March:** The dispute over the ownership of the Star church goes to court in Edmonton.

1905 **February:** The Manitoba government establishes the Ruthenian Training School for the purpose of training bilingual teachers. The school opens in Winnipeg, but in 1907 is transferred to Brandon.

1907 The Star church dispute is carried by successive appeals to the Privy Council in London, England. In June, this body rules in favour of the Russian Orthodox faction.

1909 **October:** The Training School for Teachers in Foreign Speaking Communities opens in Regina.

1911 The first Ukrainian to stand as a candidate in a Canadian election, Vasyl Holowacky, runs for Parliament as a Socialist in the riding of Selkirk, Manitoba. He is unsuccessful.

1913 **February:** The Training School for Foreigners opens in Vegreville, Alberta.
17 April: The first Ukrainian is elected to a provincial legislature. Andrew Shandro takes the Whitford, Alberta constituency for the Liberal party. All the other Ukrainian candidates, running as Independents, are defeated. Shandro is re-elected in 1915 and 1917.
Alberta Minister of Education, John Boyle, suddenly revokes the temporary teaching permits of 13 Ukrainian teachers, and puts an end to bilingual education in Alberta.

1914-18 **First World War** — Canada is at war with Austria. Ukrainian immigration from Galicia and Bukovina ceases. Ukrainians living in Canada, most of them Austrian citizens, are classified "enemy aliens" and are obliged to register as such. Some are detained in internment camps. Many of their democratic rights are curtailed, and naturalization is suspended. Only in the last stages of the war are Ukrainian men accepted into the Canadian army.

1915 The first Ukrainian is elected to the Manitoba Legislature — T.D. Ferley, Independent from Gimli.

1916 Manitoba government bans bilingual education in that province.

1918 Spanish influenza sweeps Canada. In the Ukrainian colonies the death toll is high. Bilingual education is stopped in Saskatchewan.
The Ukrainian Orthodox Brotherhood is founded in Saskatoon. Many parishes join the new movement.

1923 Smoky Lake, Alberta, is the first town in Canada to have a local government whose members are all of Ukrainian origin.

1926 The first Ukrainian Member of Parliament, Michael Luchkovich, is elected in Vegreville, Alberta.

Photo Credits

We would like to thank the Provincial Archives of Alberta, Public Archives Canada, the Glenbow-Alberta Institute, Calgary, and all the individuals who allowed us to make use of their historical photographs. The source of each historical photograph and the owners of artifacts depicted in original photographs, are indicated below.

All original photographs are by Martin Coles, unless indicated otherwise.

Cover illustration based on a photograph belonging to Mr. and Mrs. Bill Shandro, Willingdon, Alberta. Back cover photo courtesy of Mr. and Mrs. John Chahley, Smoky Lake, Alberta.

Mr. and Mrs. George Cebuliak, Edmonton: 4. Mr. and Mrs. Bill Shandro, Willingdon: viii, 6, 31, 36, 156. Mr. Steve Stogrin, Smoky Lake: 5, 116. Public Archives Canada: 12 — C-6196, 19 — C-5611, 23 — C-38706 (copyright: Page Toles, Toronto), 24 — C-5610, 30 — Dominion Land Patents, Liber 148 (R.G.15, Reel C-6049). Mr. Palamarek, Waskatenau, Alberta: 14 — trunk. Mr. and Mrs. John Chahley, Smoky Lake: 26, 42, 66, 83, 93 — costume, 96 — winder, 100, 121, 127, 131, 156. Mrs. Homeniuk, Sheho, Saskatchewan: 38. Glenbow-Alberta Institute, Calgary: 40 — NA-1000-9, 59 — NA-1794-1, 62 — NA-1794-2, 71 — NA-949-97 (RCMP Museum, Regina, holders of original negative), 74 — NA-473-1, 80 — NA-670-37, 82 — NA-670-38, 118 — NA-2497-16. Mr. Tom Predy, Smoky Lake: 41. Mr. Bill Antoniuk, Smoky Lake: 48, 76, 103, 108, 113, 123, 155. Provincial Archives of Alberta: 57 — B.705 E. Brown Collection, 81 — P.451 H. Pollard Collection. Mr. and Mrs. John Kretzul, Smoky Lake: 56 — grubhoe. Mr. and Mrs. John Korol, Theodore, Saskatchewan: 69, 97 — belt. Historical Village and Pioneer Museum, Shandro, Alberta: 67 — washboard, 85 — oil press, 94 — crusher, 108, 122 — school. Andrew, Alberta Museum: 82 — artifacts. Mrs. Dziwenka and John Dubetz, Smoky Lake: 82 — rake, 94 — carder, 99 — mousetrap. Dr. and Mrs. Strilchik, Mundare, Alberta: 85 — churn. Pakan, Alberta Museum: 85 — mill, 97 — hat. Mr. and Mrs. John Strynadka, Willingdon: 95 — carder, 99 — tool. Mrs. Warawa, Smoky Lake: 97 — embroidery. Mrs. Socholototsky, Smoky Lake: 97 — cushion. Mr. George Kozub, Smoky Lake: 99 — plane. Miss Mary Shewchuk, Vegreville: 144 — *kolach*, 151 — Easter eggs. Mrs. George Strynadka, Willingdon: 151 — Easter eggs. Mr. and Mrs. Nick Strynadka, Willingdon: 159.

Photos by Ken Predy: 82 (top right), 96 (top right and bottom), 99 (top right).